ACKNOWLEDGEMENTS

One of the greatest privileges anyone can enjoy in life is to be gifted with and surrounded by people who love you unconditionally and stand by you for the cause that you represent.

I have been blessed to have many of such people in my life!

First I want to appreciate my parents – who are the patriarch and matriarch of the Babatunde family – knowing that you are my parents has brought me untold joy and inspiration!

To all my siblings and their families; what an honour to have been linked together by divine providence!

To all the members of the Great Commission Church – World Harvest Christian Centre Worldwide. Thank you!

My special thanks to Pastor Sunday Adelaja, who I met at a critical hour and gave me all the encouragement to finish this book!

My special thanks also to many whom God has used to mentor, teach, and inspire me. They include Prophet T. O. Obadare, Pastor Shola Olukolade, Dr Paul Jinadu, Bishop Francis Wale Oke, Dr. David Shibley, Rev. Dr. Frank Ofosu Appiah, and Bishop Robert Smith Snr.

To Joshua, a leader of leaders; and the one that will lead the troops into the Promised Land!

To Grace my darling, my Prophetess in the House. What a bunch of joy and encouragement you are to me!

To the inventive genius and prophet to the nations – the weeping Prophet, J. J., the world is eagerly waiting for your manifestation!

Rev Wale Babatunde

ENDORSEMENTS

*"I am honoured to count Pastor Wale Babatunde as
one of my friends. He has a great love for this country
as his writings clearly prove. He himself has drawn
inspiration from men and women who have been
influential in the development of the British nation over
the centuries. Looking at their lives, Pastor Babatunde
writes with passion and sincerity as he highlights their
Christian convictions which he rightly perceives as the
creative dynamic that has guided the nation. He longs
to see similar spiritual power among leaders today and
he looks forward to a time when God will again bless
this nation. He believes this will only happen when
commitment to prayer and social action become the
main drivers in the church."*

The Rev Dr Clifford Hill, MA.BD.Ph.D., Issachar Ministries
Moggerhanger Park, MK44 3RW

*"These prophetic words to me represent God's agenda
for this nation; heaven will be invading these Isles
again! I suggest that you read this prophetic and
historical book as a call to arms. It points to the past
as well as the future whilst demanding action in the
present. Study this volume and be challenged. Digest
it contents and be changed. If you do not want to do
anything significant for God then don't pick up this
book! It is a must read for all leaders and Kingdom
seeking Christians."*

Dr Jonathan Oloyede
Convenor National Day of Prayer & Worship U.K

"Historical revisionism is wrecking havoc in the Western world. Pastor Wale Babatunde unearths the roots of the true greatness of a great nation. A biblically-based ethos is deeply entrenched and entwined in the heritage of Great Britain. It cannot be extracted from British life today without a callous disrespect for the nation's history that would cause immeasurable damage to its future. Pastor Babatunde is to be commended for this important work."

David Shibley, GLOBAL ADVANCE
PO Box 742077, Dallas, TX 75374-2077
www.globaladvance.org & www.davidshibley.com

"It was Aldous Huxley who once said, "That men do not learn very much from the lessons of history is the most important of all the lessons that history has to teach." This is precisely the gap Wale Babatunde is trying to bridge. Tracing the role of Judeo-Christianity in the evolution of Great Britain, the book is a wake-up call to all British citizens and all who have benefitted from this great country. At a personal level, it will point your attention unmistakably to the Lord Jesus, stirring you up to a new level of life. A must-read for all!"

Pastor Taiwo Odukoya, Senior Pastor
The Fountain of Life Church, Ilupeju Lagos

"The author W. Babatunde deals with those who brought social, economic, and religious liberty to Great Britain as well as emancipation around the world. These were people who jeopardized their lives for Christ to make a difference in their time and to change unjust laws and practices of humankind. A fascinating read to inspire men and women today to make an impact on their age."

Dr. Judy Fornara, Founder of Spiritual Life Church, Spiritual Life Bible College, and Denominational Founder of Covenant Life Ministerial Organization (Brooklyn Center, USA)

"No nation on the surface of the earth has paid so much a price for world missions than the UK. When Africa, South of the Sahara laid in darkness, it was the sons and daughters of Great Britain who dared to believe that by taking up the evangelistic mandate entrusted to them, people who sat under the shadow of darkness could experience the dawning of the grace of God. Many went with their burial clothes, knowing they were not coming back

In 1900 only 10m Africans were believers. Today, the number is 360m and the estimate is that African Christianity will increase to 1.03 billion by 2050. The writer of this book comes to you as a "harvest of the seeds" that were sown by the missionaries of Great Britain.

Wale Babatunde has a heart to see the fires of revival ignite again in the UK. His optimism about God revisiting the UK is captivating regardless of the odds that stare at us, and I totally agree with him.

The depth of apostasy in Great Britain is shocking.

The Assistant Bishop of Newcastle – The Rt Rev Paul Richardson, wrote in the Guardian Newspaper on the 29th June 2009 and said "Christian Britain is dead" and warned that the Anglican Church could be extinct in the next 30 years if nothing is done. Researching into history, he catalogues in detail the great spiritual leaders of Great Britain who impacted their generation with the Gospel and the holistic change it brought to the nation and how their legacies have lived after them. Today, the Spirit of the New Age and Secularism seeks to undo the Judeo-Christian family structure

The writer calls us to arise because the rise of relativism as a fundamental societal creed has eliminated the God of Scripture and the God of the universe from any consideration in and over the affairs of society.

Unfortunately, "our generation is lost to the truth of God, to the reality of divine revelation, to the content of God's will, to the power of His Redemption, and to the authority of His Word. This loss is paying dearly in the swift relapse to paganism

"The savages are stirring again, you can hear them rumbling and rustling in the tempo of time" – Carl F.H. Henry

The writer call us not only to take up the mantle entrusted to us by our God, but must be willing also to stand unintimidated for Biblical correctness when it crosses sword with political correctness.

The journey ahead is not bleak, but a new era of hope is about to dawn on the nation because the God of the past is the God of the present and future Great Britain can be great again as the Church humbles itself, seeks God's face in prayer and turn from her wicked ways. God is counting on us as the Church, hence this book is a must read for every Christian who believes taking risks in our generation is the key to fulfil our God given mandate.

The book is a rare treasure for all who seek to see Great Britain become great again. It is spirit inspired and scriptural.

Kingsley Appiagyei
Head Pastor, Trinity Baptist Church, London
and a former President of the Baptist Union of Gt Britain

CONTENTS

Foreword

Pastor Wale Babatunde has done it again. This is the book the worldwide Christendom had waited for, for so long.

Wale, kudos to you! You are indeed a God-sent historian.

Now we can all see the genesis of our civilization, the greatest civilization the world has ever seen. This journey was started by the Apostles, they justified their calling, as seen in the words of Apostle Paul.

> *I have therefore whereof I may glory through Jesus Christ in those things which pertain to God. For I will not dare to speak of any of those things which Christ hath not wrought by me, to make the Gentiles obedient, by word and deed, through mighty signs and wonders, by the power of the Spirit of God; so that from Jerusalem, and round about unto Illyricum, I have fully preached the gospel of Christ.*
>
> (Romans 15:17-19)

From the words of Apostle Paul it is clear that they did a good job, they did not just invade and penetrate all spheres of life, but they actually covered the whole continent of Asia and the Roman Empire for the Kingdom.

Then God entrusted the Gospel to the hands of ordinary men and women, flesh and blood from Great Britain, through whom God made Great Britain great. These men turned the whole world into a vast mission field. They did not just penetrate all spheres of society; they created the spheres and stood on top of the mountains to proclaim the Lordship of Jesus.

Today, we shall hear their stories and the secrets of their greatness in this wonderful piece of work by Pastor Wale Babatunde. I see this book as a bridge between their generation and ours. Through this book I believe the Lord wants to pass to us a baton of responsibility to reach our generation for God's purposes.

It is not enough to just go to church, no, far from it. It is not enough to just be born again, no, not at all. We must become the Christians after God's own heart, of whom it was said, "they that turned the world upside down have come to us" (Acts 17:6b).

May this book be used of God to touch the hearts of men of our generation to take up the mantle of bringing the Gospel of the Kingdom to every sphere of human endeavour.

Sunday Adelaja
Senior Pastor
Embassy of the Blessed Kingdom Of God for All Nations
Kyiv,Ukraine

Introduction

In June 2002, I felt a divine compulsion to write the book *Great Britain Has Fallen!* In this book I argued from historical facts that the very foundation and fabric of Britain's society is Christian and this was what gave it stature, fame, prestige and prosperity among the family of nations.

Furthermore, I contended that the spiritual, moral and commercial decline that we have experienced and continue to experience is attributable to our abandonment of the faith of our fathers!

I warned over ten years ago that unless we repent (starting with the Church) we are definitely on a collision course with God. I specifically mentioned that I believe God might break the pride of our nation – the economy! Today, it seems my prophecy has been fulfilled!

Again in 2005, while in the Houses of Parliament, I felt the same divine compulsion to sound the alarm and wake up the sleeping giant, the Church in Britain, about our indifferent attitude towards some dangerous trends in our society! While the manuscript of my second book, *Awake Great Britain,* was with my publishers, the events of 7/7 occurred which took in its wake the destruction of several lives and property.

Since 2005, I have carried a burden in my heart to write this book, *Men and Women Who Made Great Britain Great,* for a number of reasons. First I have discovered through research that there is so much rich spiritual heritage that Britain has, but which has hitherto been buried deep down in our foundations. I strongly believe that there has been a conspiracy, a well thought-out plan, an unholy, ungodly strategy by some minority elements in our nation to distort, delete or even deny our rich Judeo-Christian heritage, which has brought honour, status, greatness, influence and affluence, peace, progress and unparalleled prosperity to this island!

Just as in the days of Isaac, the time has come for us to revisit the wells which have been dug in the days of our forefathers, which the enemies have stopped.

> *"Then Isaac dug again the wells of water which had been dug in the days of his father Abraham, for the Philistines had stocked them up after the death of Abraham, and he gave them the names which his father had given them"*
>
> (Genesis 26:18, New American Standard Bible)

Secondly, I have written this book because we are at a critical hour in our history! We have been here before! What I see today and what I read shortly before the Great Awakening seem to be very similar! I believe that inspite of the darkness covering the land and gross darkness covering the people, a new reformation is on the horizon. It is already taking place (albeit on a small scale), which I believe will gather momentum in the coming days, weeks, months and possibly years! For me, there's no better way to serve and prepare our young reformers and revivalists than to point them to our past; to bring before them lives of the men and women who changed the course of history and be inspired by them! In a sense, this book is meant to help create a "model", albeit from a historical perspective. The purpose is to help inform, educate, and inspire the rising reformers that God is already raising, training and releasing for the coming revival and national transformation.

Furthermore, I have always believed that Britain has always had an apostolic mandate on its shoulders! We have always been pioneers and leaders in every sphere of life and human endeavour.

I hope that God will use this book also as a model for national transformation in other nations.

May I state that history has always been selective! It's impossible to write everything that needs to be written in one book! For this reason, I want to acknowledge that the choice of the men and women in this book has been personal. It does not, in any way, display that there are not many others who deserve to be mentioned!

I do hope that, one day, I or someone else might take up this challenge in looking at the lives of these unsung heroes.

CHRISTIANITY, CHRISTIANS AND THE CHURCH

1 *WHAT HAVE CHRISTIANITY AND CHRISTIANS EVER DONE FOR US?*

"For [even the whole] creation (all nature) waits expectantly and longs earnestly for God's sons to be made known [waits for the revealing, the disclosing of their sonship]."

(Romans 8:19, The Amplified Bible)

"The real voyage of discovery consists not in seeking new landscapes, but in having new eyes."

Marcel Proust (1871-1922)
French novelist, critic, and essayist

The Summer was in her usual beauty and skin-tingling persona yet again. Holidaymakers and tourists were basking in the heat and sweat typical of the season. In the midst of the bustling and boisterous crowd, he mingled. The buildings, lights and the general atmosphere were all new to him. This was his first time here. He was new to the country, alien to her peculiarities, foreign to the traditions. Though he felt odd, he knew he was in the right place. A deep-seated conviction burned deep within. Part of this conviction would be fuelled by what he saw; the people, the legacies, their history. There was something striking about them all. Slowly, the conviction gave way to a tunnel-vision commitment; a sold-out surrender to a divine mandate. Years would pass by, as the conviction gave way to a driving urge to make hay as the sun kept shining.

Yes, he had a mandate from above. He would pursue it, talk about it, teach on it.

The chronicles of this foreign land he found himself in would lead him to discover phenomenal change agents who etched milestones in the history of their birthplace. That man is me, Pastor Wale Babatunde. The land, Great Britain.

This book is about these amazing individuals who radiated the light of their faith fearlessly and unabashedly. They were the very persons who made their mark in the milestones of the country known to the world as Great Britain.

I consider myself honoured to share with you such deep insights gleaned from the social and spiritual generals who have, in part, defined the history of this country.

Allow me to introduce to you these great men and women who made Great Britain great.

Who Were They?

Many stories have been told of sterling personalities who changed the course of history in Britain through their passion and commitment to a worthy cause. They sought to influence positively the lives of citizens and residents in Great Britain. Some risked their health, reputation, and their lives (in extreme cases). However, one thread that runs through their identity is their professed faith.

I stepped onto the shores of the Island which is today known as Great Britain on the 22nd of July 1992. I had a mandate. The message was clear. Three times had I heard it. Without a doubt, it was from the Holy God, known by many as *Elyon* (Most High)!

I had barely spent a week when I noticed a number of things that were foreign to me. The first that confronted me was the apparent prosperity, far from what I had ever seen or experienced anywhere else!

I also noticed how free the nation was; the citizens, media and foreigners alike expressed their views without being intimidated, sanctioned or silenced. This I found quite refreshing, though poignant. Many countries in the world, including the African continent where I was raised, are not so liberal with the term *Freedom of Expression*!

What further caught my attention was the reception and civility that greeted foreigners. In my own estimation, Britain is one of the most accommodating nations you can ever visit or live in!

A Land and Her Identity

Consider this: Britain provides accommodation, health care, education and, often, financial benefits to foreigners unlike no other country in the world. I realized that even the most dangerous elements who find themselves on the shores of Britain enjoy most of these benefits. In their country of birth, it would likely have been an entirely different scenario.

Then, there is the welfare system and the various social reforms that have been directed towards those who deserve such support, the poor, weak, and elderly.

Who were the change agents behind these reforms and what motivated them?

These existing social and economic structures were legacies that developed over time through the pioneering efforts and relentless pursuit of phenomenal change agents. By virtue of their endeavours, lives were saved, hopes restored, purposes affirmed.

Furthermore, I was keen on finding out the particular individuals to whom were credited various scientific discoveries.

These discoveries saved millions of lives, benefitting countries around the world.

As an avid student of history, I dug further to ascertain what really propelled such fearless individuals to travel as far as Africa and certain remote parts of the world.

Could there have been more to their drive? Were there economic motives behind their drive?

The more I searched, the more questions kept burning deep within me.

Why did the missionaries come to Africa, not just with the Bible to convert the "heathen" but to do more than preach the Gospel? Why did they further seek to educate and empower through commerce as well as minister to their physical bodies through modern medicine? These and many more were questions that flooded my mind!

Another question that recurred in my mind was this: who and what were responsible for the greatness our beloved nation has attained from decades ago? Recently, someone pointed my attention to the fact that there is no other nation today that has "Great" before its name. Before then, I had never seen it in that light.

However, on second thought, I came to one conclusion. Great Britain will be considered "Great" by most of the people among the family of nations, particularly if they are conversant with her history.

May I point out that even in the midst of perceived waning of Britain's influence in the 21st century, something continues to tick. She is still, nevertheless, regarded as a 'Great' nation.

Great Britain indeed is blessed with an enviable history; she was once the leading maritime power, and also possessed some of the best educational institutions the world has ever known. The English language, without doubt, is the most widely spoken language in the world. Furthermore, the British Parliament is referred to as the "Mother of Parliaments".

From the above, the question then arises: what debt do we owe these very Christians of 'ages past'? What sterling contributions have they made to the social development and greatness of our great nation? After all, we do understand the importance of giving honour to whom it is due.

I strongly believe the hour has come for us to settle this issue once and for all, the story behind the sequence of events that led to the name 'Great Britain' and the *dramatis personae* involved.

The Clarion Call

It is my considered opinion that the time has come for all the mouths of gainsayers to be stopped. We need to know the truth. It is time that the Church, Politicians, Monarchy, Muslims, Hindus, Atheists, Agnostics, and all those who seek to deny or derogate our rich Judeo-Christian heritage, face the facts. All those who have sought refuge here from their country (including those who are bent on destroying our democratic values) must acknowledge who or what is responsible for the peace and prosperity that they have come to enjoy on our shores.

At this point, may I state clearly that I seek not to add any information that is not already known. Neither do I intend to present it in a rather different light. Rather, through the very individuals who have defined the history of this great country, I seek to draw your attention to certain inalienable facts.

These facts bear witness to how we have come to where we are. Allow me guide you through the annals of history as we observe how people and events have shaped the legacy we benefit from to this day.

In furtherance of this point, let us draw inspiration from Her Majesty, Queen Victoria, herself.

*"England has become great and happy by the true
knowledge of the true God and Jesus Christ."*
Queen Victoria in her message to two African Chiefs[1]

Observe closely to whom Her Majesty ascribed the source of Great Britain's modern day status. It was not man's political wit or economic ingenuity. It was through the knowledge of the true God *and* Jesus Christ.

Jesus Christ is the Source, the Author, Foundation and reason for our greatness. This is what happens in nations where the knowledge of Christ is rediscovered, where Christ is honoured and enthroned. The effect is peace, prosperity, riches, honour and greatness.

Trevelyan Writes

George Macaulay Trevelyan was a distinguished historian. He wrote on the 19th century revival of John Wesley and George Whitefield that dramatically changed the history of our nation. In his words,

*"It was one of the turning points in the history of
the world."*

On the abolition of the slave trade, he had this to say,

*"Her command of the sea, her far flung empire, her
mounting industrial power, her commercial supremacy,
her inventive genius- above all, her increasing moral
stature and her expanding spiritual vision- won her
a place of unique leadership amongst the nations.*

1   *The Trumpet Sounds for Great Britain*, Vol 1. David Gardner, p 97, Christian Foundation Publications, Cheshire UK, 1980

More than any other great nation in the middle of the
ninetieth century, she was worthy of world power."[2]

It is worthy of note that the greatness described above by
George Macaulay Trevelyan is a direct reference to results
of the Christian revival led by the duo of John Wesley and
George Whitefield.

A Resonating Memorial

Westminster Abbey is an architectural landmark rich in tradition
and history. In the north transept of this Gothic architecture is
an inscription to William Pitt. He was the Earl of Chatham and
the inscription reads:

> *During whose administration in the reigns of George II*
> *and George III, Divine providence exalted Great Britain*
> *to a height of prosperity and glory unknown to any*
> *former age!*

I believe our forebears placed this message in this prominent
place in our nation so that succeeding generations would take
this to heart!

Sir Timothy Hoare Speaks

Sir Timothy Hoare was one of a small group of far-sighted
individuals in the early 1960s. This group set about bringing
the Gospel to the City of London.

He was also a founder member of the evangelical group,
the Church of England's *Church Assembly* (and subsequently

---

2   *The Trumpet Sounds for Great Britain*, Vol 1, David E Gardner, pp 95-96, Chris-
      tian Foundation Publications, Cheshire UK, 1980

General Synod) to which he was elected for a total of 40 years.

He has added his voice to the voice of many who have ascribed Britain's greatness to the Christian God.

He remarks,

> *"It had been their religion, which had originally given the English that sense of being special, of being set apart by God"[3]*

Two British Prime Ministers have spoken explicitly about the role the Bible has played in our national history.

Margaret Thatcher (1979-1990, the longest serving Prime Minister) spoke in 1988 on the centrality and the impact the Bible and Christianity had made in our nation.

She declared unequivocally,

> *"We are a nation whose ideals were founded on the Bible. Also, it is quite impossible to understand our literature without grasping this fact. That is the strong practical case for ensuring that children at school are given adequate instruction in the part which the Judaeo – Christian tradition has played in moulding our laws, manner and institutions. How can you make sense of Shakespeare and Sir Walter Scott or of constitutional conflict of the seventh century in both Scotland and England without such fundamental knowledge? But I would go further than this. The truths of the Judaeo-Christian tradition are infinitely precious, not only, as I believe, because they are true, but also because they provide the moral impulse which alone can lead to that peace in the true meaning of the word, for which we all long... there is little hope for democracy if the hearts*

---

3   *Our National Life*, Allister Vale Edt, Monarch Books, p 14, 1998

of men and women in democratic society cannot be
touched by a call to something greater than themselves.
Political structures, state institutions, collective ideals
are not enough. Democracy requires the life of faith...
as much to the temporal as to the spiritual welfare of
the nation."[4]

The Right Honourable David Cameron, speaking on the 400th anniversary of the King James Bible, declared,

"The King James Bible has bequeathed a body of
language that permeates every aspect of our culture
and heritage. From everyday phrases to our greatest
works of literature, music and art, we live and breathe
the language of the King James Bible, sometimes
without even realising it. And it is right that we should
acknowledge this – particularly in this anniversary year.
Second, just as our language and culture is steeped
in the Bible, so too is our politics. From human rights
and equality to our constitutional monarchy and
parliamentary democracy...from the role of the church in
the first forms of welfare provision, to the many modern
day faith-led social action projects... the Bible has been a
spur to action for people of faith throughout history, and
it remains so today. But what I am saying is that the Bible
has helped to give Britain what it is today, values and
morals, we should actively stand up and defend..."

So, to whom do we owe most of our scientific discoveries? Who were the men and women behind our various social reforms that many of us, including my children who are originally from Nigeria, are enjoying today!

---

4   *Christianity and Conservational*, the Rt. Hon. Michael Alison MP and David I. Edwards EDS, pp 337-338, London; Hodder and Stoughton, 1990

Which people educated us as a nation? To whom do we ascribe the honour for establishing some of the most meritorious institutions in the world like Oxford and Cambridge Universities? Which people changed the lot of prisoners in this country and why? How did the game of competitive football originate?

Who were the men and women that championed the abolition of the slave trade and what place did their faith play? Who were the people behind the founding of children's homes, societies for the prevention of cruelty to animals, the Red Cross? Why did they start such groups and societies?

It is to these questions and many more that we shall be turning our attention in this book.

Making History

1. What do you consider to be your purpose on earth?
2. What conviction do you carry that keeps you going about your calling?
3. How do you live each day? With anticipation or dread of the unknown?
4. What is that one thing you are willing to live for and if necessary lay down your life for?

2 *THE MANDATE OF THE CHURCH*

‖‖‖‖‖‖‖‖‖‖‖‖‖‖‖‖‖‖‖ ‖‖

"Each generation of the church in each setting has the responsibility of communicating the gospel in understandable terms, considering the language and thought-forms of that setting."

Francis August Schaeffer,
American Presbyterian Pastor (1912-1984)

"Now I say to you that you are Peter (which means 'rock'), and upon this rock I will build my church, and all the powers of hell will not conquer it."

(Matthew 16:18, New Living Translation)

Why does the Church exist? What functions are we supposed to be fulfilling on earth today? What mandate did Christ leave His Body to accomplish before He comes to rapture His Church? What major role is the 21ˢᵗ century Church meant to play here and now?

I am of the strong opinion that our theology often determines our practices. What we believe rightly or wrongly affects our actions. For example, why will some kill and maim in the name of God? The answer is simple; it's their theology.

Historically speaking, the Church of Jesus Christ has been divided into two camps:

1. **The Evangelicals**: The mandate of this camp has traditionally been hinged on the following passages. They include:

"Go ye therefore and teach all nations, baptizing them in the name of the father, and of the son, and of the Holy Ghost, teaching them to observe all things whatsoever I have commanded you, and lo, I am with you always even unto the end of the world."

(Matthew 28:19-20, KJV)

"And he said unto them, Go ye into the entire world and preach the gospel to every creature. He that believeth and is baptized shall be saved, but he that believeth not shall be dammed. And these signs shall follow them that believe, in my name shall they cast out devils, they shall speak with new tongues, they shall take up serpents, and if they drink any deadly thing, it shall not hurt them, they shall lay hands on the sick, and they shall recover."

(Mark 16:15-18, KJV)

"And said unto them, Thus it is written and thus it behoved Christ to suffer, and to rise from the dead the third day. And that repentance and remission of sins should be preached in His name among all nations, beginning at Jerusalem. And ye are witnesses of these things."

(Luke 24:46-48, KJV)

"Then said Jesus to them again, peace be unto you, as my father hath sent me, even so send I you."

(John 20:21, KJV)

"But ye shall receive power after that the Holy Ghost is come upon you and ye shall be witnesses unto me

both in Jerusalem and in all Judea, and in Samaria
and unto the uttermost part of the earth."

(Acts 1:8, KJV)

The above passages (known as the Great Commission passages) are all derived from the command of Christ to the Church. They constitute the marching order to take the Good News of God's Kingdom to the ends of the earth! As a result, there are groups within the Body of Christ that believe the primary reason for our existence on the earth today is the proclamation of the Gospel. The ultimate aim is the conversion of sinners and drawing back the lost into God's Kingdom. Many Evangelicals traditionally hold the view that this is our most important assignment, conversion of souls. I must confess that after over twenty five years of preaching the gospel, I subscribe absolutely to this school of thought.

2. **The Liberals**: Christians who belong to this camp believe in and are totally committed to social action. It is worth pointing out that there are many groups under this label. One extreme belongs to those who believe the mandate of the Church is to be "do gooders" and not proclaim the Gospel. Their theology is hinged on the fact that *"Actions speak louder than words. That our good works will or should attract people to the Lord."* Some of the passages that this camp base their practice on include James 2:14-17 (KJV):

    "What doth it profit my brethren, though a man say he hath faith, and have not works? Can faith save him? If a brother or sister be naked and destitute of daily food and one of you say unto them, depart in peace, be ye warmed and filled, notwithstanding ye give them not those things which are needful to the body, what doth it profit? Even so faith if it hath not works is dead, being alone."

Again in Matthew 25:35-40, KJV:

> "For I was hungered, and ye gave me meat, I was thirsty
> and ye gave me drink, I was a stranger and ye took me
> in, naked, and ye clothed me, I was sick and ye visited
> me, I was in prison and ye came unto me. Then shall
> the righteous answer Him saying, Lord when saw we
> thee an hungered, and fed thee? Or thirsty and gave
> thee drink? When saw we thee a stranger and took
> Thee in? or naked, and clothed Thee? Or when saw we
> Thee sick or in prison and came unto Thee? And the
> King shall answer and say unto them, "Verily I say unto
> you, in as much as ye have done it unto one of the
> least of these my brethren, ye have done it unto me."

The positions of both do have some validity in their claims,
as they are both based on Scripture. Interestingly, these two
camps have (over the years) shaped the manner in which the
mandate of the Church has been pursued.

Need For Balance

Aerodynamic technology focuses on how air interacts with
moving objects. A key objective in this regard is attaining
balance; in flight, for instance. This is why airplanes have two
wings, to attain balance. I believe this is what we need in the
Body of Christ. To subscribe to just one of the above schools,
as many have done for centuries, is to simply look at one side
of the coin and ignore the other.

The proclamation of the Gospel and the practice of Christian
piety are simply two sides of the same coin. To do one without
the other is an incomplete gospel.

Writing in the same vein on the twenty first century challenge
in her inspiring work, *Redeeming Our Communities*, Debra
Green remarks,

*"These social reformers from years gone by have
inspired millions of Christians to follow in their
footsteps, and yet the surface remains only slightly
scratched. Why is this? Well one reason is that we're
not really sure where we stand biblically in terms of
our understanding of the gospel. Many Evangelical
Christians have been taught that "doing good works"
is not only unnecessary, but may even be a distraction
from the really important task of preaching the gospel.
Traditionally, "social action" has been the province
of "Liberals". Those who considered themselves "true
Christians" would prioritise the need to proclaim and
explain the gospel so that individual sinners could
come to repentance and faith. Thankfully, this dualism
between the preaching and practice of the gospel is
rapidly fading into the background. Only a tiny minority
of Evangelicals still cling to the old definitions. Most, if
not all, of today's Evangelistic organisations embrace
a more balanced and holistic view as do most church
denominations and streams. There is a new generation
of believers emerging that don't even know there's
an issue"[5]*

I believe a great number of men and women under discussion in
this book embraced a holistic and balanced view of the Gospel.
They were not just content with proclaiming the Gospel. They
further embraced and demonstrated their vocation, mission and
ministry in the world as being "salt and light". They did not just
embrace evangelism, but were interested in the evangelisation
of the communities they found themselves in. They were not
only interested in the people, but they concerned themselves
with the structures of the society they lived in. This is probably
the missing link in our gospel today.

5   *Redeeming Our Communities*, Debra Green, p 31, New Wine Press, Chich-
     ester, UK, 2008

Making History

1. What is your conviction about preaching the Gospel, liberal, evangelical or both?

2. The Bible is your Source. How much time do you devote to your Source for nourishment and empowerment?

3. The demands of everyday living can take their toll on a person's drive to preach. What is your approach to dealing with balancing the need to preach and live a fulfilled life?

3 *THE GOSPEL OF THE KINGDOM*

"Vision is the art of seeing what is invisible to others."
Jonathan Swift (1667-1745),
Anglo-Irish essayist and cleric

*"Faith is to believe what you do not yet see; the reward
for this faith is to see what you believe."*
Saint Augustine of Hippo (354-430),
Bishop and Philosopher

A meaningful understanding of the lives, activities and
contributions of the men and women under study in this
book will be difficult without exploring what the Gospel of
the Kingdom truly means. This is largely because the term
"Kingdom of Heaven" was well understood by these unique
men and women. Conversely, 21st century Christians need some
inspiration in order to live out our faith in the way they did.

When Jesus began His earthly ministry, He announced the
beginning of God's reign. His kingdom (or rule) had come.
When He preached, He declared,

"Repent for the kingdom of heaven is at hand."
(Matthew 4:17, NKJV)

John the Baptist, Jesus' cousin and forerunner, came also with the same message as he also declared,

> *"Repent for the kingdom of heaven is at hand."*
>
> (Matthew 3:2, NKJV)

It is worth mentioning that there are 137 references to "the Kingdom" in the New Testament *corpus* and over 100 of these are during Jesus' ministry. His entire teaching and approach as Messiah (the *Saviour-King*) centre on this theme.

What is "The Kingdom"?

The Kingdom refers to God's Sovereign rule in the universe. He is the King of the Heavens. But more specifically, when it is used in the Gospels, it refers to the entry of God's long-anticipated Anointed One, the promised Son of David, who would not only be the Saviour, Deliverer, and King of Israel, but of all mankind. Finally, the rule of God's King was about to overthrow the power and rule of all evil.

Matthew, the Gospel writer, had a particular understanding of the Kingdom. To him, the Kingdom consisted of at least three elements:

1. **THE PERSON OF THE KING**

   There's no kingdom without a king. Every kingdom is ruled by a monarch. In this instance, Jesus is the much awaited King; not only of the Jews but also the Gentiles. This is why Matthew skilfully crafts the genealogy of two important Jewish personalities. One is David, their ideal king. The other is Abraham, the founder of the Jewish religion. Furthermore, Jesus' genealogy is traced to include the Gentile in the person of Rahab, a prostitute. Therefore, as Jesus is our King, Christians are citizens of the kingdom.

We are Royalty (1 Peter 2:9). It is for this reason that when we study the Gospel, we are primarily studying about our King, King Jesus. The purpose of studying the King is to imbibe His nature and character, that our integrity as citizens can be studied and understood by all.

2.   THE POWER OF THE KINGDOM

"The Spirit of the Lord is upon me, because He has anointed me to preach the gospel to the poor; He has sent me to heal the broken-hearted. To proclaim liberty to the captives and recovery of sight to the blind. To set at liberty those who are oppressed. To proclaim the acceptable year of the Lord."

(Luke 4:18-19, NKJV)

The Kingdom came not only with the person of the King, but also Kingdom power. Jesus came to demonstrate Kingdom power to release mankind from every form of oppression of the devil. This can be seen from his inaugural manifesto; *liberty to the captives, recovery of sight to the blind and liberty to all those who were oppressed* (Isaiah 61:1-3). It is worth mentioning that deliverance here is not just limited to the healing of physical abnormalities. It further extends to liberty or justice for the oppressed, downtrodden and the socially disadvantaged. This was why the Gospel of Luke specifically declares in the Beatitudes, *Blessed are you poor...* in Luke 6:20 (NKJV) as opposed to Matthew, *Blessed are the poor in spirit* (Matthew 5:3 NKJV). For the same reason, Matthew devotes a section on his account to the demonstration and manifestation of Kingdom power. See Matthew 5:1, where He began His healing, deliverance or power ministry. Any lesson for 21st century ministers and ministries? I strongly believe there is a lot to learn in this regard. Our ministry should not only cover learning, studying or teaching about the person of the kingdom. This ministry of ours will be incomplete without the demonstration of Kingdom power. After all, Jesus declared in Mark's gospel (Mark 16:17-18, NKJV),

> *"And these signs will follow those who believe: In my name they will cast out demons; they will speak with new tongues. They will take up serpents; and if they drink anything deadly it will by no means hurt them; they will lay hands on the sick and they will recover."*

It was the understanding of this dimension of the Kingdom that defined the character of Smith Wigglesworth, one of Britain's most illustrious sons and a household name.

> *"And my speech and my preaching were not with persuasive words of human wisdom, but in demonstration of the spirit and of power, that your faith should not be in the wisdom of men but in the power of God."*
>
> (1 Corinthians 2:4-5, NKJV)

The early Church operated in the power of the Kingdom. Read the book of Acts and see for yourself. Why do you think it was called the "Acts of the Apostles"? Observe closely repeated and recurrent demonstrations of power, the occurrence of signs, wonders and miracles on a daily basis.

Take a look at the ministry of Moses. He had to demonstrate to Pharaoh and Egypt (and even Israel) that he had been sent by God. Moses' question to God about the authenticity of his mission and mandate is very instructive.

> *"Then Moses answered and said, "But suppose they will not believe me or listen to my voice, suppose they say, the Lord has not appeared to you."*
>
> (Exodus 4:1, NKJV)

What was God's response? Signs, wonders and miracles! He was to demonstrate Kingdom power through the various plagues.

Our demonstration of power is meant to authenticate our message that we have been commissioned by the King. This is why a section of the Body of Christ that denies the place of healings, miracles, signs and wonders is not only in delusion, but preach at best a half-baked, incomplete and impotent gospel.

3.   THE PRINCIPLES OF THE KINGDOM

When Jesus came to inaugurate the Kingdom, He did not just come with power. He also came with some principles or new teachings to live by. As Jesus announced the Kingdom, He came as the second Moses, the Law Giver of the New Kingdom who came to deliver the laws of the Kingdom. Notice the parallel between Jesus and Moses. Both of them were not only teachers or law givers, but they both climbed the mountain before they delivered their message.

Moses' Ten Commandments instructed the Jewish nation on how they were to first relate to their King (God) and next to fellow citizens. The same applied to Jesus in the Beatitudes or BE-HAPPY-ATTITUDES, where He laid new rules or laws of the new Kingdom which is not limited by geographical, racial or ethnic boundaries.

Adherence to these new laws is meant to attract or serve as a witness to those outside the Kingdom because we are now living under a superior law or principle. This is the reason why the teaching ministry is so vital to the success of the Great Commission. Jesus declared,

> *"Teaching them to observe, all things, whatsoever I have commanded you."*
>
> (Matthew 28:20, NKJV)

The lifestyle of Kingdom principles demonstrated by the early believers made them to be identified as Christians in Antioch.

The Two Dimensions of The Gospel Of The Kingdom

By the grace of God I have preached the gospel in different parts of the world, in the last twenty five years. I must have preached a few thousand messages. However, the most revolutionary revelation I received from the Lord over these years is what I am about to share with you. This was what motivated the Christian men and women who changed the history of Great Britain. Without this fact, the essence of this book will be lost. It is the understanding and practice of this truth that is lacking in the Church, both in Britain and most parts of Europe today.

This revelation is the missing ingredient in the Church within Africa. There is need for our information base to be fine-tuned or updated from time to time. A lot of ministers and believers today need to experience an expanded view of the Gospel of the Kingdom. Let's consider the testimony of the Bible.

"Now a certain Jew named Apollos, born at Alexandria, an eloquent man and mighty in the scripture, came to Ephesus. This man had been instructed in the way of the Lord and being fervent in spirit, he spoke and taught accurately the things of the Lord, though he knew only the baptism of John. So he began to speak boldly in the synagogue. When Aquila and Priscilla heard him, they took him aside and explained to him the way of God more accurately."

(Acts 18:24-26, NKJV)

A lot of us need an in-depth revelation about the Gospel of the Kingdom. I have often wondered at what I would personally label as an oddity. Why is it that despite the ever increasing numbers of those who profess to be Christians in Africa (particularly the West African sub region), coupled with the growth of ministries and the attendant growth of ministers, there is hardly such demonstration of power as recorded in the Acts of the Apostles? This is not to mention the staggering financial resources at our disposal, the political influence and capital that Christians wield (This is not ignoring certain ministries that are operating mightily in Kingdom power to the glory of God).

In the light of the above, there is still such a pathetic and pervasive state of affairs, economically, socially and morally. The answer is this: a sizeable percentage of Christian ministers and followers seem not to understand the message of the Kingdom and its implication. Get ready for information, inspiration and revelation that is bound to change your life forever!

The First Dimension Of The Gospel Of The Kingdom: The Gospel Of Salvation

"And she will bring forth a son and you shall call His name Jesus, for He will save His people from their sins"

(Matthew 1:21, NKJV)

The first thing about the Gospel of the Kingdom is that it brought with it salvation to sinners. It should be pointed out that in Greek terms, when we speak of salvation, it is an encompassing word. It means wholeness, deliverance, healing and prosperity. Therefore, when Jesus came to save us, He brought wholeness, healing, prosperity and deliverance. It must be stressed that the gospel of salvation is the entrance point into the Kingdom.

Here Lies the Problem

As stated earlier, I have often wondered why, despite the multiplicity of churches and ministries around the world (particularly in Africa), we are still finding it difficult or impossible in changing or transforming our societies. The simple reason is that our gospel has been limited to the Gospel of Salvation.

Take a look at the following and closely observe these references:

1. The content of most Christian TV programs
2. The subject of most Christian teaching and preaching
3. The theme or thrust of most Christian conferences and gatherings
4. The subject of most Christian books, tapes and resources

I guarantee you this; at least 95% of our focus is on the Gospel of salvation, healing, deliverance, prosperity and protection. What this does is to turn God into Father Christmas. Anytime we come for fellowship, we are coming with our shopping list. This is the main reason why the average 21st century believer is very self-centred, thereby building a self-cult. Again, this is one reason why a high percentage of church members are bound in a church building and are often very immature and flaky.

This, to me, is the main reason for the high level of moral decadence that I observe in mainly African countries that are filled with millions of Christians and so many churches.

The Second Dimension Of The Gospel Of The Kingdom: The Social Gospel

"Then one of them, a lawyer, asked Him a question; testing Him and saying, 'Teacher, which is the great commandment in the law?' Jesus said to him, "You shall love the Lord your God with all your heart with all your soul and with all your mind. This is the first and great commandment. And the second is like it: you shall love your neighbour as yourself. On these two commandments hang all the law and the prophets."

(Matthew 22:35-40, NKJV)

Perhaps the best way to explore this subject is to define first what the Social Gospel is. The term was an early 20th century Protestant Christian movement which placed its emphasis on the application of Christian principles to society's problems. Until this time, most Protestant ministers did not do much to address any of the growing problems of industrial society.

However, as the 19th century closed, rapid urbanization and industrialization convinced many Protestant clergymen that there was a need for them to promote certain ideals of social justice which could be derived from the Gospels. Although it made use of a number of ideas from Europe, the movement was almost entirely American, characterized by a buoyant idealism and pragmatic action-oriented program.[6]

The earliest examples of the development of the Social Gospel can be found in the teaching of Solomon Washington Gladden in the 1870's. Gladden urged his parishioners to apply the Gospel in addressing the many problems which faced residents in the slums of Columbus, Ohio. Later, during the

---

6   http://atheism.about.com/western-social gospel.htm

violent strikes which occurred in 1877, he worked to bring labour and business leaders to a peaceful agreement.

You can see from the above that the Gospel of Salvation focussed on the individual relationship with God and the meeting of their personal needs and, sometimes, greed. The Social Gospel focuses on the needs of the community or our neighbours. Thus the importance in Jesus' answer, when He was asked about the greatest commandments,

> *"You shall love the Lord your God with all your heart with all your soul and with all your mind."*
> (Matthew 22:37, NKJV)

It is very instructive to note that Jesus connected and equalled the love for our neighbours with the love for God with *all of our heart, strength and soul* (emphasis mine). Therefore, it is impossible to love God and not love our neighbours. According to James, our faith is dead without works (*James 2:26*), good works. Christians are meant to be "Salt" and "Light" in the world and not in the Church.

Dr A. B. I. Olowe, in his monumental work *Missions Reformation*, has further elaborated on this. He writes,

> *"The two times Moses received the 10 Commandments, God gave him on two slabs of stone, Exodus 34:1; it was intentional. God separated the laws relating to God from those relating to men. This means that the gospel of God is two gospels combined into one."[7]*

The first Gospel (the Gospel of Salvation) makes one 'self-centred'. The second (the Gospel of Good Works or the Social Gospel) makes one 'other-centered'. This, in itself, is the thrust or basis of Christianity. Here lies the reason why the Church

7   *Missional Reformation*, A. Olowe, p 131, Omega Publishers, Houston, USA, 2009

has not completed the Great Commission. This is why I call what is being preached in many churches and nations today the incomplete Gospel. Without this missing ingredient, I don't think the end will come. Jesus declared to us one of the critical signs that will precede the close of this age.

> *"And this Gospel of the kingdom will be preached in all the world as a witness to all the nations and then the end will come."*
>
> (Matthew 24:14, NKJV)

You might ask why I have gone to this length to give all these details about the various components of the Gospel of the Kingdom. What correlation does all this information have with our subject title?

Let me point out a few observations.

1. The exceptional men and women who made Great Britain great had a firm understanding of what the Gospel of the Kingdom meant. They did not just limit their revelation to the Gospel of Salvation; they applied or lived out their love for God by showing piety for their fellow humans. What else do you think inspired William Wilberforce and the Clapham sect in their desire for the abolition of the slave trade? What do you think made William Booth champion the cause of the poor, the downtrodden in the East End of London such that they adopted the motto, "Heart to God, Hand to Man"? Why do you think Elizabeth Fry devoted all her energy and resources towards the lot of prisoners in England? What do you think was responsible for Mary Slessor fighting for and stopping the killing of twins in Calabar, Nigeria? The desire to obey the injunction, "...love thy neighbour as thyself".

2. Secondly, I have lived and ministered in the United Kingdom for over 22 years, and I have seen many godly,

faithful and committed servants of God labour night and day to change the spiritual landscape of Britain and many parts of Europe. Unfortunately, they have largely been unsuccessful, particularly in reaching the indigenes and bringing about national transformation. What I believe is missing in this regard is the Gospel of the Kingdom.

3. Thirdly, and probably more importantly, there seems to be a "spiritual contradiction" taking place in many parts of the African continent. There are many well-meaning Africans who are concerned about the phenomenal growth and the number of Christians, churches and Christian ministry in the African continent yet we seem to be far from any national transformation. I am a Nigerian, a very proud one at that. Just like many nations in Africa, Nigeria has witnessed phenomenal growth in numbers, churches and ministries alike. We have witnessed the largest number of Christians in every sphere of our society up to the highest political offices in the land. Yet, there are many despicable things happening in this great country of my birth. Why? I believe the Church is yet to fully embrace the Gospel of the Kingdom.

Landa Cope lamented on this perplexing problem facing the African continent, in spite of the fact that Africa is the most evangelized continent. The poor people in most of the African states where "Christians" have taken roots are becoming poorer. Her submission is that we are today reaping the harvest of preaching salvation alone at the expense of salvation and good works. She writes,

> "The message that reformed western cultures and built nations on solidly Christian values was not the gospel of salvation, but the gospel of the kingdom, which includes salvation. The truth of the gospel of the kingdom is to transform us as they teach us how to live every part

> *of our life. Our transformated lives are then to be salt*
> *and light to our families, neighbors, communities and*
> *finally our nations making them better places to live*
> *for everyone. Not perfect communities; not heaven on*
> *earth but better because the influence of good is as*
> *great, if not greater than evil."[8]*

Herein lies the key to understanding the message of this book. All the men and women who made Great Britain great in different spheres changed as a result of the Gospel of Christ. They, in turn, decided to change the lot of their neighbours and society. This is the great need of this hour.

.

8   Ibid, p 136

Making History

1. Faith is key in living a life of Kingdom power. How do you build your faith?

2. Reaching out to others presents the opportunity to demonstrate Kingdom power. Do you nurse any fears or hindrances? What are they and why?

3. Living a life of Kingdom power demands a life of integrity, amongst others. What are you when no one is looking?

4. What do you understand to be the gospel of salvation and the social gospel?

5. Can you identify any social need in your community that can be used to minister the love of God to them?

6. Can you highlight three important things you have learnt in this chapter and how you intend to integrate them into your life?

4 THE GREAT MEN AND THE SPHERES OF SOCIETY

"If we are to go forward, we must go back and rediscover those precious values – that all reality hinges on moral foundations and that all reality has spiritual control."

> Martin Luther King, Jr. (1929-1968),
> American Civil Rights Activist and Clergyman

"If you are working on something exciting that you really care about, you don't have to be pushed. The vision pulls you."

> Steven Paul "Steve" Jobs (1955-2011),
> American Entrepreneur and Founder of Apple

My first two books, *Great Britain Has Fallen* and *Awake Great Britain*, aptly capture my admiration for Great Britain, my country of adoption.

I first landed on the shores of Britain on the 22nd of July 1992. It did not take me long before I fell in love with the country. Though my attention was much captivated by what I saw, what stood out was the myriad of Christian-based legacies imprinted on every sphere of British society. In addition the air of prosperity pervaded the economic landscape.

Unlike many nations I had visited, the systems running the country were well ordered. In addition, there was discipline, citizens were catered for and foreigners were treated with civility like in no other country I had previously visited. It was in Britain that I first observed that the government provided education, accommodation, health care and social amenities for foreigners. These provisions were further extended to illegal immigrants and even suicide bombers!

What could have been responsible for this? Why is Great Britain regarded as a great nation among the family of nations? Who were the men and women that brought about this status, and what motivated them? Are there lessons one can glean today from their lives and their activities? All these issues and questions raced through my mind for many years. As I began to study and travel around the country, the answers began to flood in.

First, I discovered that it was transformed men and women, those who had accepted Jesus Christ as Lord and personal Saviour, who brought about these changes on the British Isles. They believed it was their Christian duty to bring about the betterment of society and indeed the world they lived in. To them, to believe in the Gospel of the Kingdom and leave the world the way they found it was untenable.

Secondly, I found out through my research that the individuals (the subject of this book) never limited their activities or scope to the religious sphere. They never nursed a poverty mentality neither did they exhibit an escapist theology. They believed that God is the Creator of this world. Preaching an authentic Christian Gospel, in their estimation, meant positively impacting their society and indeed the world. This was why they provided education, devised scientific inventions beneficial to mankind, and were involved in politics and government in order to live under just laws and societies.

They championed social reforms, led the way in philanthropy and started football clubs in order to combat social problems of their day. Christians were the ones who led the way in the media, first through the printed pages and then the electronic media as late as 1933. This was when the British Broadcast Corporation was dedicated to Christ!

The first commercial banks on this island were started and run by Christians, their mission and vision all rooted in Christian principles. Many of our best known and oldest business concerns were actually run by Christians.

The Seven Spheres of Society

It therefore goes without saying that their activities and missions influenced different segments of society, apart from the religious, as I have pointed out earlier. My thoughts and understanding only became crystallized when I first came across the book *The Seven Mountains Prophecy*.

In this book, Johnny Enlow highlights what he calls the 'Seven Mountains' that the end time Church must infiltrate and possess with Kingdom culture. This strategy will usher in the Second Coming of Jesus Christ. He further gives the Church a blueprint on how Christians can fulfil their vocation in the world, to be the salt and light.

In order to fulfil the Great Commission in discipling nations, we need to conquer "seven nations greater and mightier than you". These seven nations were the nations that Israel was supposed to conquer before they possessed the Promised Land.

> *"When the Lord your God brings you unto the land which you go to possess and has cast out many nations before you, the Hittites and the Girgashites and the Amorites and the Cannanites and the Perizzites and the Hivites and the Jebusites, seven nations greater and mightier than you."*
>
> (Deutronomy 7:1, NKJV)

According to the theory propounded by Johnny Enlow, these seven Old Testament nations that Israel was meant to conquer now represent Media (Hittites); Government (Girgashites); Education (Amorites); Economy (Canaanites); Religion (Perizzites); Celebration; arts, music, sports, fashion, entertainment (Hivites) and Family (Jebusites).[9]

The Loren Cunningham and Bill Bright Model

It is vital to mention that this seven-mountain strategy was originally given to two modern day generals in the Lord's army – Loren Cunningham of Youth With A Mission (YWAM) and the late founder of Campus Crusade, Bill Bright.

As both men were on their way to meet each other for a scheduled meeting, the Lord separately gave them the same revelation, "a Seven-Mountain Strategy". Discipling nations was what these men and women understood to be the key to fulfilling the Great Commission.

Finally, since history serves many functions which include to instruct, inform, and inspire us, I am including this piece of information in order to rouse my generation to action. I believe this chapter and indeed this book can act as a model, a prototype for us to learn from the lives and activities of our forebears. The ultimate aim is towards spurring us to finish the Great Commission. After all, one of the redemptive gifts of Britain is apostolic, to act as a catalyst or a forerunner.

9   *The Seven Mountains Prophecy* Johnny Enlow, Creation House, Florida, USA, 2008

*"Now all these things happened to them as examples
and they were written for our admonition, upon whom
the ends of the ages have come."*

(1 Corinthians10:6a, NKJV)

Making History

1. There are so many misleading influences in the media. How are you lending your voice to correct such deception?

2. Where do you believe you fit in as regards the seven mountain strategy and conquering these areas for the furtherance of the Gospel?

3. Emerging and existing trends in every facet of living have influenced Christian living negatively and positively. How has this affected you?

4. Can you identify what you need to do in order to become a voice to be reckoned with in your sphere of influence?

5. No one person is created to solve everyone's problem. Have you identified your passion and calling?

THE SPHERE OF EDUCATION

5 EDUCATION IN ENGLAND
How did it all begin?

"Get wisdom. Get understanding"

(Proverbs 4:5, NKJV)

"Study and be eager and do your utmost..."

(2 Timothy 2:15, The Amplified Bible)

Perhaps the greatest obstacle to the emergence of popular education in England was the twin evils of slavery and the slave trade. As long as both were allowed to flourish, it was impossible for any humanitarian or social reform to take place, including popular education.

Education Before The Evangelical Revival

It should be pointed out that prior to the evangelical revival and its attendant impact, general education for the populace was already in operation. The only institutions, however, where it was operating were Charity Schools, privately endowed schools, Dames' schools and a few struggling institutions. These struggling institutions were run by non-conformists to save their faith and independence from utter extinction.

The Charity Schools, under the control of the Church, were meant for the poorest of the poor in society.

Dames' Schools, on the other hand, were private ventures conducted in private houses, sometimes by spinsters, in poverty.

The rich and the privileged, on their part, educated their children either by private tutors at home or at one of the great boarding institutions known as public schools. So how did the English popular educational system begin?

J. Wesley Bready has asserted in his book, *England Before And After Wesley*, that there were at least six separate and distinct phases in the development of England's popular educational system. They are:

1. Sunday School Movement
2. The Royal Lancastrian Institution (later the British and Foreign School Movement)
3. The National School Society
4. The Factory Schools
5. The Ragged School Union and finally,
6. The Famous Board School Act of 1870, supplemented by the Acts of 1876 and 1880, established universal and compulsory education throughout the land[10]

What is important for our present work is that the foundation of popular education in England is completely Christian. This should be noted by all and sundry. It was changed men and women who had a relationship with Jesus Christ who laid the foundation of popular education. It has been asserted that the establishment of the Sunday School by Mr. Raikes of Gloucester was the beginnings of popular education in 1780.[11]

It is also worth mentioning that in 1769 Hannah Ball, with the support of Wesley, had established a flourishing Sunday

10   *England Before And After Wesley*, 1938 p 353, Hodder & Stoughton, London
11   Ibid, p 353

School in conjunction with her day school in High Wycombe. Silas Told, the life friend of criminals, had on Sundays long taught poor children at Wesley's Foundery, London, to read the Bible.

So successful was this Sunday School system that by 1786 no less than 200,000 English children were regularly attending Sunday Schools. By 1831, when Lord Shaftesbury unveiled a statue to Raikes, it was claimed that already in Great Britain alone 1,250,000 children were attending Sunday Schools.[12]

I sincerely yearn that God would raise up new movements similar to the Sunday Schools that will be so relevant and life transforming that they will sweep all across this nation!

It should also be mentioned that Lord Shaftesbury occupies a great position in his contributions to the development of popular education in England. He fought for social reforms through the various Factory Acts, which sought to protect underaged children from factory tyranny. In addition, his campaigns for the establishment of Factory Schools and Ragged Schools are well documented.

Perhaps the best picture of the origins and what motivated the establishment of the popular educational system in England can be found from the question raised by Sir Thomas Chambers. After the advent of Board Schools he remarked,

> *"Who are they that have brought about this marvellous improvement in the amount of education given, and in educational machinery involved? Who but the members of all the Evangelical churches throughout the country? Who have filled the Sunday schools, and the Ragged Schools and to a great extent the National Schools, with teachers?"*

---

12   Ibid, p 354

It is important that we all pay attention to the answer Sir Thomas Chambers gave in this regard.

Let all Christians, Muslims, Buddhists, Hindus and all our politicians take note of this answer.

> *"Who but the men who have acted from religious*
> *motives, and whose conduct has been influenced by the*
> *teaching of the Gospel?"[13]*

Let the record be set straight once and for all. Let this be made clear for posterity to read. Practical religion, by this I mean the Christian faith, pioneered the movement for popular education in England. It further interjected purpose, power and poise into the very concept of education.

As noted earlier, the moral and spiritual decline which was in progress at this time had inevitably caused education to reach an extremely low ebb, prior to the great revival. A very high percentage of both adults and children could neither read nor write.

It was when the revival came and the spiritual awakening spread that there was a longing in the hearts of men and women to read the Bible. It was this longing that Wesley and others set themselves to satisfy.

Wesley encouraged his converts to teach themselves how to read. He also made good use of the printing press to provide his converts with good Christian literature. Thus, the curriculum of the early schools was very simple, reading and writing as well as knowledge of the Bible.

So successful was the Sunday School Movement that George III, a promoter of the revival, gave the movement an additional push. In 1805 he made his famous statement,

"It is my wish that every poor child in my dominion shall be taught to read the Bible."[14]

---

13   Ibid, p 361
14   *The Trumpet Sounds for Great Britain*, Vol 1, David E Gardner, p 84, Christian

When in 1870 the School Board Acts were passed, they had as their purpose,

> *"To complete the voluntary system and to fill up the gaps, but not to supplant the voluntary system."*[15]

Oh that our MP's, Ministers of Education, and our Prime Minister take note of this. Let all pastors, Christians and Christian educators please take note. Britain owes it to the Eighteenth century revival of Christianity that she had a system of popular education.

Christians should be reminded all over this nation about the unique contribution to the greatness of this nation. It is my opinion that it is because we have abandoned our responsibility in the field of education that our nation is in its appalling state.

It is because we have left out Bible instruction from our school curriculum that we have a whole generation of children behaving in an antisocial manner. It is because our lawmakers have tried to destroy the foundation of our educational system built by our fathers. They have succeeded in kicking out God, the Bible and prayer from our schools and public places. This is one of the reasons we are breaking records of evil practices all over Europe.

In my research I also came across some interesting findings which need to be preached and pondered on. In an age such as ours, we have tried to destroy or in many cases deny our rich Christian heritage because of political correctness. Did you know that the most famous educational institutions in this country that have produced the great men, the pride of this nation, all had Christian foundations?

Foundation Publications, Cheshire UK, 1980
15   Ibid, p 84

Eton College

Without doubt Eton College has educated many great men for more than five and a half centuries after its foundation. The famous institution has the enviable fame of being second to none.

The College, a pride of this nation, has succeeded in distinguishing itself as one of the important citadels of learning across the globe. Little wonder then that it has produced some of the best brains and most influential personalities.

For example Robert Boyle "the father of Chemistry" was educated at Eton. Eton has also produced nineteen Prime Ministers in Great Britain, and one Prime Minister of Northern Ireland. Eton has further produced great writers such as Thomas Gray, Percy B. Shelly, Henry Fielding, Aldous Huxley and George Orwell. Great economists include John M. Keynes while old Etonian explorers were Sir Humphrey Gilbert, founder of the colony of New Foundland, and Captain Oates, who was on Scott's expedition to the South Pole. Perhaps what is not acknowledged openly or what the secular humanists have tried to gloss over is the fact that Eton was originally founded as a Christian College. The founder was King Henry VI. His vision was a Christian College from the very beginning. This fact is obvious from the institution's structure, curriculum and activities.

Another fact peculiar to Eton College was that at its foundation there was a community of priests, ten of them Fellows. In addition, there was a pilgrimage church and an almshouse. Also, at the inception, fourteen Christian services were held each day. As a daily practice, the boys woke up at 5am, first with prayers. No food was allowed the students on Fridays, as this was a day of fasting. All these point to the fact that the foundation of this famous college, which has produced great men that made Great Britain great, is completely Christian. It should not also be forgotten that in Medieval times, the word "College" meant *a community of priests* rather than *a place of education*.

I have been reliably informed that recently Eton College appointed its first Imam in the history of the institution.[16]

This to me is a shame for a college which began purely as a Christian institution. This is one of the ways in which we have been eroding and destroying our Christian education.

Matters that border on faith and religion require some level of sensitivity and tact as can be gleaned from historical records. In present times, such an appointment might not be perceived as a matter that can raise any dust. However, in the light of the legacy and heritage of this great institution, such an appointment throws up some questions.

One of such questions is this: how many Muslim schools have a pastor as a member of staff, employed to propagate the Christian faith?

Oxford And Cambridge Universities

I have decided to write about Oxford and Cambridge for a number of reasons. First and foremost, both universities have earned reputations throughout the world for being exceptional centres of academic learning.

Oxford and Cambridge Universities both rank as leading universities in the world. It is as a result of this fame that William Camden has written about Oxford what PomPonius Mela says of Athens,

   'it is too well known to be pointed out.'[17]

Oxford University, which started during the 1100's, is the oldest university in Great Britain. Without doubt, it is one of the most famous institutions of higher learning. Cambridge, on

---

16   *The Daily Telegraph*
17   *A History of Christian Education,* Paul A. Kienel, Association of Christian Schools International, Colorado Springs 1998

the other hand, is said to have started in 1209. These premier universities have brought fame and greatness to this nation, an undisputable fact.

It is for this reason that the alumni converge yearly from all over the world to attend these universities' reunion events, because of their track record. Again, both universities have made Oxford and Cambridge key tourist cities in the United Kingdom. However, what many may not know today is that the foundations of the universities were designed for Christian intents and purposes.

In my research I discovered that both universities actually started out as training institutions for the clergy.

Our oldest, most famous and perhaps the best universities started out as Bible Colleges.

Mark Curtis, writing about the transition that took place in these universities from purely a theological training institution to where lay professions and public bureaucracies were taught, remarks,

> "...from having been training grounds for the clergy,
> they (Oxford and Cambridge) became training schools
> for the lay professors and public bureaucracies."[18]

In my research I was also reliably informed that in the early days of both universities whoever was not a signed up communicant could not be admitted into these universities. Put differently, the initiation service for new students was the Holy Communion. I hope our present educators and students of these great universities, past and present, will thank God for inspiring and raising up Christians who established these premier institutions.

There is yet another piece of evidence about the Christian foundations of these institutions. The first College in Cambridge

18   Ibid, p 351

University, Peterhouse, was founded in 1284 by Hugo de Balsham, Bishop of Ely.

Making History

1. As a history maker, what are you doing personally to promote Christ centred education?

2. As a pastor, elder or board member, can you write out an educational policy for your local church or denomination that will make it compulsory for your church or ministry to be actively involved in Christian education?

3. A challenge to Africa – the missionaries came from Britain and other European countries and offered us free and high quality education! Many of such schools still exist today! With the vast financial resources in many churches in Africa, how can we redress the problems of providing expensive Christian education even to some of our members?

6 *FLORENCE NIGHTINGALE* *Education and nursing*

||||||||||||||||||||||||||||| |||||||||||||||||||||||||||||||||||||||||||||||||||||||||||||||||||||||||||||||||||

"From the beginning of the war, Nightingale's popularity with the British public had been enormous because of the letters that the soldiers wrote to family and friends about her and the articles in the Times that described her tireless work on behalf of the sick and wounded. As word of her accomplishments spread, she became a kind of national heroine-cum-saint in Britain and beyond."

Extract from the book, Florence Nightingale,
Barbara Montegomery Dossey, RN, MS HNC, FAAN
Pioneer of Holistic Nursing Movement

"It is said that she did an amount of work which big and strong men were unable to do. She used to work nearly twenty hours, day and night. When the women working under her went to sleep, she, lamp in hand, went out alone at midnight to the patients' bedside, comforted them, and herself gave them whatever food and other things were necessary. She was not afraid of going even to the battle-front, and did not know what fear was. She feared only God. Knowing that one has to die some

day or other, she readily bore whatever hardships were
necessary in order to alleviate the suffering of others."
Extract from the Indian Opinion, 1915,
Mohandas Karamchand Ghandi (1869-1948),
Indian Nationalist and Civil Rights Activist

There are few women in English history who tower higher than
Florence Nightingale. She was born on the 12th of May 1820
at the Villa Colombia near the Porta Romana at Bellosguardo
in Florence, Italy. Her family was a rich upper class and well-
connected British family. She died at the age of 90 years on the
13th of August 1910, in Park Lane, London, United Kingdom.
She was laid to rest in the churchyard of St Margaret Church,
East Wellow.

Religious Background

Florence Nightingale was a firm believer in God. By this, I mean
the God of Abraham and the father of our Lord and Saviour,
Jesus Christ. This is particularly important for many reasons.

First, we live in an age when God is ridiculed in the
media. Conversely, rising to the heights typical of Florence
Nightingale and still being associated with God usually
earns one some form of public ridicule. Let the secular
humanists please take note. Let all our modern day nurses
never forget this: the mother of modern nursing was not an
atheist or humanist.

Her Call Into Ministry

Like the erudite scholar from a very influential background,
Saul of Tarsus, Florence Nightingale had a definite call into the
nursing profession which I believe was her sphere of influence.

In February 1837 she received this call while at Wembley
Park. It must be said that this decision was at great cost; her
mother and sister were stoutly against this decision.

Their reaction was more because of their status and the expectations they had of her being a wife and a mother. Despite their reaction, she stood her ground.

This is so important for us to understand, as she took a stand against the accepted norm of her life. It must also be added that pioneers and history makers are people who do unconventional things.

Furthermore, another price she had to pay to fulfil her call was to reject the offer of marriage. As far as she was concerned, marriage would interfere with her ability to follow her calling as a nurse. She was courted by many potential suitors like politicians and writers. Among such persons were poet Richard Monckton Milnes and 1st Baron Houghton. She rejected them both and many more.

Later she had strong relations with Benjamin Fowett who may have wanted to marry her, but it never happened.

Florence Nightingale was a much travelled woman. One of the experiences that would mark a turning point in her life occurred while she was abroad, near Cairo. She wrote in her diary,

> *"God called me in the morning and asked me would I do good for him alone without reputation?"*[19]

This statement reveals, amongst many others, two things about Florence Nightingale.

First, it again showed how deep-seated her faith was in the God of the Bible, the God of our fathers, not the foreign gods that have invaded our country today.

Secondly, and possibly more importantly, her calling was to do good on behalf of God. She never sought to do anything for her own reputation.

---

19   Wikipedia

In other words, she made up her mind to be selfless like her master Jesus. The only person that was to be famous through her work was God.

I believe there's a lot present-day Christians can learn from her decision. Our calling and ministry in the public arena should only result in God and not ourselves being famous. We must, like Nightingale, become people of no reputation.

Her Contributions

"She is a ministering angel, without any exaggeration, in these hospitals, and as her slender form glides quietly along each corridor, every poor fellow's face softens with gratitude at the sight of her when all Medical officers have retired for the lamp in her hand, making her solitary rounds."[20]

Christians are called by God to be change agents. We are called not just to love God with all of our mind, heart and strength and afterwards be imprisoned in our churches week after week. We are further expected to love our neighbour as ourselves.

Our love should always possess an outward working towards our neighbours.

It was in light of this that Jesus declared to his followers,

"You are the salt of the earth.... you are the light of the world.."

(Mathew 5:13, 14 NKJV)

"For we are his workmanship, created in Christ Jesus unto good works which God hath before ordained that we should walk in them."

(Eph 2:10, NKJV)

Florence Nightingale had a particularly strong conviction; it was impossible to love God and not serve fellow humans. This was what motivated her.

The Crimean War

Her most outstanding contributions came during the Crimean war, particularly when reports began to reach Britain about the pathetic condition of the wounded soldiers. What was Florence Nightingale's response? In October 1854, she and a staff of thirty-eight women volunteer nurses trained by her, sailed across the Black Sea to Balaklava in the Crimea where the main British camp was situated.

What was the condition she met? Her party found soldiers being badly cared for by overwhelmed medical staff in the face of official indifference. Medicines were in short supply, hygiene was being neglected and mass infections were common, many of them fatal. There was no equipment to process food for the patients.

At the beginning of the 20th century, it was asserted that Nightingale reduced the death rate from 42% to 2% either by making improvements in hygiene herself or by calling for the sanitary commission.[21]

As a result of her experience during the war, she came up with the idea that most of the soldiers died more through poor living conditions, than those killed on the battle front. As a result of this unique finding, Nightingale helped reduce deaths in the army during peace time and turned attention to the sanitary conditions of hospitals.

Nightingale spent a great deal of her life in pioneering and developing the nursing profession and organising all its modern form. She helped raise about £45,000 by 1859. This

21   Wikipedia

was used to set up the Nightingale Training School at St Thomas Hospital on the 9th of July 1860. It is now called the Florence Nightingale School of Nursing and Midwifery and is part of Kings College London.

She also wrote a 136-page book titled *Notes on Nursing* which served as the cornerstone curriculum in the school.

Other contributions of this great woman include being a pioneer in graphical representation statistics, part of which is the pie chart now known as the polar area diagram.

"Like a fiery comet, Florence Nightingale streaked across the skies of 19th century England and transformed the world with her passage. She was a towering genius of both intellect and spirit, and her legacy resonates today as forcefully as during her lifetime."

Extract from "Florence Nightingale"
by Barbara Montegomery Dossey

Summary Of Her Contribution

1. Established the first official training programme for nurses in Britain in 1860.

2. Set an example of compassion commitment to patient care, diligent and thoughtful hospital administration.

3. Her lasting legacy led to the establishment of the Florence Nightingale Declaration campaign by nursing leaders throughout the whole world. This was facilitated through the Nightingale Initiative for Global Health which aimed to build a global grass roots resolution for adoption by the U.N. General Assembly in 2008.

It was therefore in view of her great contributions to the greatness of Great Britain and indeed the world that an offer

was made to bury her in Westminster Abbey. However, the offer
was declined by her relatives.

Making History

1. What are you ready to give up in pursuit of a dream
   or vision?

2. How far are you willing to go towards making life better for
   your neighbour or fellow human being?

3. What risks are you prepared to take in pursuit of
   your dream?

7 THOMAS SYDENHAM
The father of English medicine

"You are the light of the world. A city set on a hill cannot be hidden."

(Matthew 5:14, English Standard Version)

"What you are is God's gift to you.
  What you do with yourself is your gift to God."

Danish Proverb

Throughout this book, I have tried to argue one thing; modern Britain would never have gained premier status among the family of nations but for the inventions and contributions of men and women who had been changed by the glorious gospel of Jesus Christ. Thereafter they considered it their sacred duty, through the compassionate spirit of Jesus, to affect and change the lot of their fellow humans.

Such was the 17th century English physician known as the "English Hippocrates" and the father of English medicine, Thomas Sydenham. He was born at Wynford Eagle in Dorset, and later on schooled at both Oxford and Cambridge. He also fought in the British Civil War with his father and two brothers on the side of Oliver Cromwell.

Thomas Sydenham (1624-1689) left a lasting legacy in medicine. This was partly because he inaugurated new methods and better ethics of practice. He was held in such high esteem by his fellow professionals that Hermann Boerhaave, the Leyden Professor, wouldn't even speak of him in his class. He rather referred to him as "The light of England, the skill of Apollo, the true face of Hippocrates."[22]

Some of his contributions to modern medicine include the following:

◊   The introduction of opium into medical practice.

◊   The first person to use iron in treating iron-deficiency anaemia.

◊   Popularising the application of quinine in treating malaria.

It was particularly as a contributor to medical therapy that Sydenham acquired his reputation. Furthermore, his moderate treatment of smallpox, use of cinchona and his invention of liquid laudanum all came to symbolise his greatest contributions to medicine. His renown also came from the fact that he alleviated the suffering of the sick and made all his patients well.

What is vital for us to take note of is that Sydenham's passion as a pioneer in medicine was not just for rational, experimental, scientific or material gain. His primary concern was for the glory of God and the love of his fellow human beings. It must also be echoed that the Bible, the best inspired, best literature ever, undergirded Sydenham's medical mission. He summarized his medical philosophy in the following advice to his students when he remarked,

"Whoever applies himself to medicine should seriously weigh the following considerations. First, that he will one day have to render an account to the Supreme Judge of the lives of sick people entrusted to his care.

Next, by whatever skill or knowledge he may have,
by the divine favour become possessed of should be
devoted above all things to the glory of God and the
welfare of the human race. Thirdly, he must remember
that it is no mean or ignoble creature that he deals
with. We may ascertain the worth of the human race.
For its sake God's only begotten son became man
and thereby ennobled the nature that he took upon
him. Finally, the physician should bear in mind that
he himself is not exempt from the common lot, but is
subject to the same laws of mortality and disease as his
fellows and he will care for the sick with more diligence
and tenderness if he remembers that he himself is their
fellow sufferer."[23]

Making History

1. Your chosen field of endeavour or job is your place of influence. How unique are you when you are at work?

2. What are you doing differently that is making a difference in your career or place of work?

3. Are you adding value in the lives of those at your workplace and community through your work or career?

4. What inspires you the most from the life of Thomas Sydenham?

23   *The Works of Thomas Sydenham*, Thomas Sydenham, MD, Preface to 1st edition, 1666, translation R.G Lutham, p 25, Sydenham Society, 1848

8 MEN OF SCIENCE – MEN OF GOD

"I know of no more encouraging fact than the unquestionable ability of man to elevate his life by a conscious endeavour."

Henry David Thoreau (1817-1862),
American author, poet, and philosopher

"You can tell what they are by what they do."
(Matthew 7:16, Contemporary English Version)

No one will ever question the importance or significance of science to modern man. Scientists over the past centuries have contributed in no small measure to the survival and wellbeing of mankind. From Leonardo da Vinci to Robert Boyle, to the Age of Isaac Newton and William Ramsay, we owe a great debt to these great scientists of the past. It is without controversy that Great Britain has produced some of the best scientists whose contributions have not only benefited this country and Europe but the whole world.

One thing that I, however, found interesting is that majority of the best scientists and bright minds whose contributions and significance have spanned generations and nations were not only born in this country, but they were Bible-believing Christians. This, I believe, is a fact that present day secular humanists refuse to acknowledge. However, I think the moment of truth has come for us to acknowledge the place of God in this country's greatness. I do challenge all peoples of various religious persuasions and those who subscribe to the various dogmas, ideologies and 'isms', it's time to dig out the facts.

Francis Bacon (1561-1626)

The Lord Chancellor of England is usually considered to be the man primarily responsible for the foundation and establishment of the now popular 'scientific method' in science. He stressed experimentation and induction from data rather than philosophical deduction in the tradition of Aristotle. Bacon's writings are also credited with leading to the founding of the Royal Society of London. Again, like Sir Isaac Newton, Francis Bacon was a devout believer in the Bible. He wrote,

> *'There are two books laid before us to study, to prevent our falling into error; first the volume of the scriptures, which reveal the will of God, then the volume of the creature which expresses His power.'*[24]

I hope the next time the name of Francis Bacon is mentioned in our schools, the Royal Society of London, or any institution in this land for that matter, will acknowledge that he was a devout Christian and a great believer in the Word of God. In addition, he believed that the Bible was relevant and sufficient for mankind as far as life and godly living were concerned.

---

24   *Men of Science Men of God*, Henry M. Morris, pp 13-14

Robert Boyle (1627-1691)

Robert Boyle was another Briton considered in his time to be probably the greatest physical scientist in his generation. He is credited with being the father of modern chemistry. His name is associated with the basic laws he discovered, through which he related gas pressures to temperature and volume, the fundamental principle of gas dynamics. He was also one of the founders of the Royal Society of London.

Yet, this great scientist was a humble, witnessing Christian and a diligent student of the Word of God. He was greatly interested in missionary enterprise and as such devoted much of his money to Bible translation work and the propagation of the Gospel. He was strong in apologetics, funding via his will the Boyle Lectures for proving the Christian religion.[25]

Michael Faraday (1791-1867)

The history of great scientists of all time will be incomplete without the name of Michael Faraday, universally acknowledged as one of the greatest physicists of all time.

He was especially gifted in scientific experimentation, particularly in developing the new sciences of electricity and magnetism. He discovered electromagnetic induction and introduced the concept of magnetic lines of force. He further invented the generator and made many other key discoveries and inventions, yet this man of humble background was a sincere Christian. He was very regular and faithful in the various ministries of his church, both public and personal. He fully believed in the official doctrine of his church. In his words,

25   Ibid, p 16

> *"The Bible and it alone, with nothing added to it nor taken away from it, is the sole and sufficient guide for each individual, at all times and in all circumstances. Faith in the divinity and work of Christ is the gift of God and the evidence of this faith is obedience to the commandment of Christ."*[26]

Faraday today would be considered a New Testament believer. However, he would be regarded as one of the greatest scientists of all times.

Isaac Newton (1642-1727)

Isaac Newton is universally acknowledged as one of the three most influential scientists in history. So great was this man's contribution that it is no exaggeration to say that almost everything we do in the modern world is based on Newton's enormous scientific achievements.

So popular was Newton in this nation that his funeral ceremonies were akin to those typical of national heroes. On the day he was laid to rest, the pall bearers included the Lord High Chancellor, two Dukes and three Earls. This in itself meant a lot. His monument in Westminster Abbey had been previously reserved for England's greatest nobility. No such honour had ever been given to a man of science. Such was the influence of this man that someone once wrote:

> *"It is said Newton had a greater influence on the world than had any mortal with the exception of another prophet...Mohammed. His memory has been immortalized*

---

by poets and historians. To a remarkable extent the
greatest of scientists had the gift of prophecy."[27]

So what was this great scientist known for? Isaac Newton is famous for, among other things, his discovery of the Law of Universal Gravitation, the formulation of the three Laws of Motion which made possible the discipline of dynamics and all its subdivisions, and his development of calculus into a comprehensive branch of mathematics, now a basic tool in every science. He anticipated the great Law of Energy Conservation, developed the Particle Theory of Light Propagation, and as an astronomer constructed the first reflecting telescope.

However, one thing that the secular humanist will prefer to overlook about this great scientist is that he was a genuine Christian from his youth. It was said of Newton,

> *'...he knew more about the Bible, Church history and*
> *prophecy than all of England. His library was rich in*
> *books of theological interest. He studied the Bible daily*
> *and was a firm believer in its authority...'[28]*

On charity and piety Newton was very generous, paying for the distribution of Bibles to the poor and supporting friends and others who came to him in need.

It should be noted that even though Newton's reputation rests on his scientific work, prophecy occupied Isaac Newton's interest for a relatively long period of his life. Even while he was finishing his monumental *principia* at age 28, he had grown tired of science and became engrossed in interpreting the book of Daniel which had fascinated him since his youth. Over the

---

27   *Observations on Daniel and the Apocalypse of St. John,* Isaac Newton, http. ww.historicist.com/Newton/title.htm
28   *The Protestant interpretation of Bible prophecy, the historical alternative* http//www.historicist.com/Newton/title.htm

remainder of his life, he would write over 1,300,000 words on religious subjects with prophecy as his principal focus.

I believe there is a great lesson that modern scientists and secular humanists must learn from the 'father' of modern science on science and faith. For Newton, science did not contradict faith, but supplemented and enriched it. Exploring God's creation was a way of becoming sensitive to the glorious workings of a God whose illimitable creative powers were everywhere evident, but nowhere fully explicable.

For those who try to disprove the existence of God through science or those who think God is not relevant in modern times, now is the time to learn from our Father. It is time we go back to our foundation, the Rock from which we have been hewn.

Today a lot of scientists not only deny the existence of God, but they deny creation as being His handiwork. Newton writes,

> "This most beautiful system of the sun, planets,
> and comets is not to be attributed to some blind
> metaphysical necessity, (but) could only proceed from
> the counsel and dominion of an intelligent and powerful
> being, (who governs all things), not as the soul of the
> world, but as Lord over all."[29]

Again we have seen that the 'best' brain in the field of science and one that has brought fame and name to Great Britain almost like no other, was indeed a believer in the Lord Jesus Christ!

---

29   *The Teacher Of Common Sense*, http://www.virtualmuseum.ca/exhibitions/annodomini/theme-15/en/theme15-1.htm

Making History

1. Your gifts and talents are meant to improve the lives of those in your community and wherever you find yourself. How much time do you devote to developing your gifts?

2. Science is for the glory of God and not to deny His power as Creator. Do you believe?

3. Does science help you appreciate or doubt God?

THE SPHERE OF POLITICS AND GOVERNMENT

Chapter 9
Lord Shaftesbury *The great emancipator*

Chapter 10
Baroness Cox *21ˢᵗ century Wilberforce or voice for the voiceless*

9 *LORD SHAFTESBURY The great emancipator*

||||||||||||||||||||||||||| ||||||||||||||||||||||||||||||||||||||||||||||||||||||||||||||||||||||||||||||||||||||||||

"You must be the change you wish to see in the world."
Mohandas Karamchand Ghandi (1869-1948),
Indian Nationalist and Civil Rights Activist

"A man can do all things if he but wills them."
Leon Battista Alberti (1404-1472),
Italian author, priest, and philosopher

Lord Shaftesbury's achievements *vis-a-vis* the greatness of Britain were many and varied. His greatest and most enduring achievements were in social reform.

In 1833, Lord Shaftesbury's Bill was, unfortunately, defeated in the House of Commons. The government, nevertheless, accepted that children needed to be protected.

For this reason a proposal was forwarded, which eventually became the 1833 Factory Act passed on the 29th August. Under this new legislation, it became illegal for children under the age of nine to work in textile factories.

Lord Shaftesbury also helped set up what was then known as the Children's Employment Commission. Its first report on mines and collieries was published in 1842. The aftermath of this report caused great sensation and anger among the British population as most people were grossly ignorant that children and women were employed as miners. Later in the same year, Lord Shaftesbury championed the Coal Mines Act through the House of Commons. As a result, women working underground were prohibited from working in such places.

Again as I read through the achievements of this great emancipator, I am confronted with a number of burning questions, "Where are the Christian social reformers of our day?" "Why are our present Christian politicians not walking in the footsteps of their forebears?" Another question that lingers in my mind is this: are Pastors and Church leaders actually training, grooming and releasing their members to serve in public life or are we simply imprisoning them within the four walls of our churches?

I cannot but raise the same questions for African countries. These are countries where faithful Christians go to church every week with many Christian politicians, businessmen and women, yet with little or no social reform happening.

Africa, where are your social reformers? Where are the likes of Shaftesbury taking up their place in history?

For many years, Lord Shaftesbury campaigned for the reduction in the hours that children worked in factories. To accomplish his aims, he used many strategies, one of which was receiving published works on the issues he was trying to change. This initiative on its own can serve as a template for aspiring social reformers.

In 1863, he also published a report revealing children as young as four and five years old still working from six in the morning to ten at night in some British factories. Needless to say, such reports sparked outrage amongst the British populace.

Once more I am greatly challenged as I read his exploits and I cannot but ask myself again, 'Where are the Shaftesbury's of my day? Where are those that will heed to the cries of the outcasts, the poor and downtrodden?'

Where are the modern day Good Samaritans? Unfortunately, just like in the days of the Good Samaritan, we have the 'Priests' and 'Levites' who are too busy with "religious" duties to attend to those who have been wounded, marginalised and left for dead by the 21st century thieves.

Lord Shaftesbury also championed other social issues. He campaigned vigorously for the provision of education for the working class. For over forty years, he was the chairman of the Ragged Schools Union. On the 4th of August 1840, Lord Shaftesbury remarked in the House of Commons,

> *"The future hopes of a country must, under God, be laid in the character and condition of its children. However right it may be to attempt, it is almost fruitless to expect the reformation of its adults, as the sapling has been bent, so will it grow. The first step towards a cure is factory legislation. My grand object is to bring these children within the reach of education."[30]*

Lord Shaftesbury did not only push for social reform, but he also pushed the Word of God. He was President of the British and Foreign Bible Society from 1851 until his death in 1885. He wrote of the Bible Society,

> *"of all societies this is nearest to my heart...Bible Society has always been a watchword in our house"[31]*

I am sure that only a few in our nation today are aware of the fact that the statue of Eros (though officially titled the Angel of Christian Charity) erected in Piccadilly Circus London in 1893 is a memorial to the monumental and unparalleled work of Lord Shaftesbury. It is a befitting tribute to all he did and accomplished as a Christian to obtain the emancipation of his fellow humans from unjust and inhuman working conditions.

---

30   www.spartacus.schoolnet.co.uk/Irashley
31   Wikipedia

This statue depicts an arrow of Christian love, piercing the world which is what Shaftesbury's love for his fellow men sought to attain.

Again, in order to leave an enduring legacy and testament to Shaftesbury's contribution to the greatness of our nation, Gladstone's tribute to Shaftesbury is inscribed round the base of his memorial in London. It reads,

> *"During a public life of half a century he devoted the influence of his station, the strong sympathies of his heart and the great power of his mind to honouring God by serving his fellow men, an example to this order a blessing to his people and a name to be by them ever gratefully remembered."*

Making History

1. To pursue a dream demands perseverance. How much staying power do you have? How far are you willing to go in order to build it?

2. Pointing out flaws in existing statutes places a demand on being versed in Law and Statutes. How much of a reader are you?

3. A heart of service is a heart of humility. How humble are you?

4. Do you feel a call to the political sphere? How much time, resources and energy do you expend here or do you permanently stay in the confines of your home and church building?

10 BARONESS CAROLINE COX
21st century Wilberforce or voice for the voiceless

"I seem to spend half my life in a jungle, a desert or half way up a mountain."

Baroness Caroline Cox Founder Humanitarian Aid Relief Trust (HART)

"Your lives are echoing the Master's Word...The news of your faith in God is out. We don't even have to say anything anymore – you're the message."

(1 Thessalonians 1:8)

The Message

It was in the summer of 1996. A middle-aged woman had been invited by the church that I lead in South–East London. She was to speak about some of her experiences and the activities of the organisation that she worked with, Christian Solidarity.

As someone raised in Africa with a Pentecostal and Charismatic background coupled with a great passion for the spread of the Christian Message, I was obviously expecting a talk that would be fiery. I eagerly anticipated something that would propel me to spread the Good News with more vigour.

I was however to be mistaken. She turned out to be a calm, soft-spoken, and knowledgeable personality. Her command of Scripture was not in doubt and she travelled widely.

The audience listened in rapt attention for one hour as she spoke. The focus of her talk was creating awareness about potential missions to certain parts of the world. She spoke about the plight of those persecuted because of their faith, individuals who were being marginalized and some trapped behind closed borders. They required urgent help, they needed to be heard.

She told moving stories of her encounters, from Sudan to Timor Leste, Uganda to Egypt, Nigeria to Burma, India to Armenia and Nagorno-Karabakh.

You might be wondering who this woman could be. She is Caroline Cox. Born on the 6th of July 1937 as Caroline Anne McNeill Love in Hertfordshire, the daughter of a surgeon co-author of an internationally renowned textbook known as 'Bailey and Love'.

She became a state registered nurse at the London Hospital from 1958, and a staff nurse at Edgware General Hospital from 1960.

In 1959 she married the love of her life, Dr Murray Newall Cox. In 1997 he passed on.

She took the title *The Baroness Cox of Queensbury* in Greater London after her peerage was announced on the 15th of December 1982, on the recommendation of the then serving Prime Minister, Margret Thatcher.

Later, in 1986, she became a Deputy Speaker of the House of Lords, a position she occupied till 2006.

Humanitarian and Human Rights Campaigner

In 1807 the slave trade was abolished. By 1833 the Act to abolish the slave trade in the British Empire came into force. As a result, it was the expectation of William Wilberforce and abolitionist groups that slave trade and slavery in general would soon become history.

As a result of the Abolitionist Act, today several international conventions seeking to outlaw slavery and human trafficking have passed and enforced various international laws.

However, despite various Acts passed among world bodies, slavery is far from eradicated. It is stated that there are more people caught up in slavery today than at any time in the history of mankind. Some estimates put the figures at approximately 27 million men, women and children.

Needless to say, the trauma involved takes its own toll on the people being enslaved, as well as their respective families and communities they come from.

I count myself very privileged. I was raised in a stable and loving home, fortunate not to have been caught up in the sinister web of slavery. It has been over two decades since I took up residence in the United Kingdom. I consider it one of the safest places to live on the planet. Furthermore, fundamental human rights are not only entrenched in the statute books, but also guaranteed and protected by various government agencies.

Without doubt, living in Britain has shielded me and many more from the untold sufferings of the marginalized. Who will speak on behalf of these untold millions? Who will be a voice to the voiceless?

This is where Caroline Cox comes in. Without any fear of contradiction, this saintly woman could be described as the 21st century William Wilberforce. Just as William Wilberforce did in the 18th century, the lot fell on Caroline

Cox to bring the attention of the British government to the horrific plight of many entrapped in modern day slavery. Again, like Wilberforce and the Clapham sect, Caroline Cox is a woman not given to speculation. She hardly took any man's word for the truth. Rather, she would investigate the facts for herself and then bring them to the attention of the whole world.

Much of what is known about the carnage in Darfur today has been brought to our attention, often at the risk of her life. Let's consider this story to drive home the point.

"The racist Islamist Sudanese government had given China unfettered access to their oil in exchange for money and weapons. The government bought bombers, assault helicopters and armoured vehicles. They funded the brutal JanJaweed Militia to kill civilians who were not Arabs, to rape women and to steal lands, goods and herds of livestock.

Caroline reached Bahr-el-Gazal with a cameraman, and found that, just days before, the National Islamist front had swept through, slaughtering unarmed men and enslaving women and children. Bodies were piled high, rotting. We went to an area of sheer carnage – human bodies, cattle, corpses, burned homes, scorched-earth policy"

They found a Christian Catechist wandering in the desolation. He had seen his church attacked; his brother and brother-in-law killed and his sister captured as a slave.

Standing in the dust of his destroyed farm, he described the men paid by the Sudanese Government to kill his people. Then he hesitated, trying to explain the worst thing "we feel completely on our own, you are the only Christians who have even visited us for years." Then he asked "doesn't the church want us anymore?"

First-Hand Experience

Anyone conversant with Baroness Caroline's family, educational and societal pedigree will agree with me that she is no ordinary person. A political figure of high repute, her educational achievements are second to none.

When people climb the success ladder in our days, what many do is to shield themselves from the realities of life.

Caroline's *modus operandi*, however, is different. She has never lost her common touch. One of the qualities that distinguish her work is her frequent travels to some of the most deprived, dangerous regions in the world, places, regions and nations that even the bravest of men will shudder to visit.

Caroline Cox has travelled several times to gain firsthand knowledge and evidence, meeting those who have suffered some of the worst injustice in the world. No wonder in one of her speeches I heard her remark,

"We don't just believe in miracles, we rely on them!"

A True National Patriot

Recently I was reading an article on Political Correctness and how it is almost destroying British politics. By the way, how can we describe Political Correctness? It has been defined in various ways as:

◊   Doing the reverse of what common sense would suggest
◊   Inconveniencing the innocent while making life easier for the wrongdoer
◊   Changing the language where you perceive it may offend
◊   Favouring a minority just for a political reason and not telling the truth in case it offends![32]

---

32   *Political Correctness – the awful truth,* ww.webring.org/hub=real political

I am a Nigerian by birth, but British by adoption. I have lived in Britain for over two decades. All my children were born here and this wonderful nation has provided for me over this period. I am eternally grateful. However there is something that upsets me about British society; not being able to speak honestly and directly about a topic or an issue. In the name of being politically correct, we have allowed our nation to be set on the path of destruction. Present times bear witness to the fruits of this misleading stance.

How many people in Britain are oblivious of the fact that radical Islam is one of the greatest threats to modern Britain? Could we say that our politicians are unaware of the steady "radicalization" of the Muslim population in Britain?

Who is ignorant of the fact that radical Islam is incompatible with our values, democracy and how our nation is in grave danger of being destroyed? Yet, how many of our politicians are speaking out? Who is placing the interest of nation above political sentiments? Who is holding Islamic leaders in our nation to account, to speak out expressly against this cancer destroying the fabric of our society?

Caroline Cox is indeed a national patriot. She is not afraid to speak the truth as it is. She stands her ground firmly, even though this may put her life at risk. Listen to her comment when she was interviewed by a Jerusalem-based journalist on the compatibility of the Islamic legal code and western Society.

> *"Sharia law is not compatible with the Universal Declaration of Human Rights; it does not allow freedom to choose and change religion; you can become a Muslim, but if you stop being a Muslim and you convert out, you run the risk of the death sentence for apostasy. It does not permit equality before the law, as between men and women, Muslims and non-Muslims"[33]*

33   Free Republic, www.freerepublic

Again speaking on the same issue, she remarked in a leading newspaper article.

> *"We cannot sit here complacently on our red and green benches while women are suffering under a system which is utterly incompatible with the legal principles upon which this country is founded."*
>
> The Independent – Baroness Cox

> *"if we ignore wrongs, we condone them"[34]*

This, I must add at this point, in no way indicates that all Muslims in Britain are radical. Many of them are good citizens.

Making History

1. Technology of the 21st century makes it possible to reach millions through the internet. How much awareness are you creating about those who need to be heard?
2. As a citizen, do you speak out against what you perceive as policies that don't protect your interest or do you just assume the politicians have it all figured out?
3. The perpetration of slavery and human trafficking still persists in the 21st century. Are you aware of it or not? What do you believe should be done about it?
4. If you feel a call into politics why not take the first step of registering with and identifying with a political party?

SOCIAL REFORMERS
AND ADVOCATES

11

THE CLAPHAM SECT
A model for
reformation
and national
transformation

|||||||||||||||||||||||||||||| |||||||||||||||||||||||||||||||||||||||||||||||||||||||||||||||||||||||||||||||

"When there is no prophetic vision the people cast off restraint."

(Proverbs 29:18a, New English Translation)

"The parish of Clapham where Wilberforce lived became the most influential parish in England. Never have the members of one congregation so greatly influenced the history of the world. The effect of their prayers and actions not only profoundly altered the religious and social life of this country, it was also felt in Africa, in the West Indies, in India and in Australasia."[35]

I have decided to add this chapter about the Clapham Sect, as they have been fondly remembered, for a number of reasons. First, I believe they are a model of what God can accomplish through committed Christians in a nation, a group united with

---

35   *The Wilberforce Connection*, Clifford Hill; Monarch Books, 2004, p 47, Oxford

one voice and a singular purpose to honour God and change their society.

Secondly, it seems history is always being repeated. From all my research, the religious as well as the socio-economic atmosphere in the later part of 18th and early part of the 19th century were very similar to what obtains today in the 21st century. Therefore, I believe there's a lot we can learn from history. After all, the purpose of history is to not just to educate and inform, but also to be inspired.

So, who were members of the Clapham Sect? They were influential like-minded individuals, members of the Church of England. They were people you could call 'social reformers', based in Clapham, London from around the 1790's to 1830's. The historian, Stephen Tomkins, has described them as a network of friends and families in England, with William Wilberforce as their "centre of gravity". They were powerfully bound together by their shared moral and spiritual values. They were further bound by their religious mission and social activism, their love for each other and by marriage.[36]

One of the most remarkable things about the group is the balance of professional skills and experience within the group, a lesson worth noting for the rising 21st century reformers. This, no doubt, helped them use their expertise and experience for advancing the Kingdom of God in the market place.

Observe the list below:

◊ Henry Venn (1725-1797), founder of the group, father of John Venn and Great-Grandfather of John Venn (originator of the Venn diagram)

◊ Thomas Fowell Buxton (1786-1845), MP and brewer

◊ William Dealtry (1775-1847), Rector of Clapham and Mathematician

◊ Edward James Elliot (1758-97), Parliamentarian

36 *The Clapham Sect: How Wilberforce Changed Britain,* Tomkins, Stephen, Oxford: Lion, 2010

◊ Thomas Gisbourne (1758-1846), Clergyman and Author

◊ Charles Grant (1746-1823) Administrator and Chairman of the Directors of the British East India Company

◊ Zachary Macaulay (1768-1838), Estate Manager and Colonial Governor

◊ Hannah More (1745-1835), Writer and Philanthropist

◊ Granville Sharp (1735-1813), Scholar and Administrator

◊ Charles Simeon (1759-1836), Anglican Minister and Promoter of Missions

◊ James Stephen (1751-1834), Master of Chancery, Great-Grandfather of Virginia Woolf

◊ Lord Teignmouth (1751-1834), Governor-General of India

◊ Henry Thorton (1760-1815), Economist, Banker, Philanthropist and MP for Southwark

◊ John Venn (1750-1830), Rector of Holy Trinity Church, Clapham

◊ William Wilberforce (1759-1833), MP successively for Kingston-Upon-Hull, Yorkshire and Bramber, Leading Abolitionist

As I read through the names of this group, I am immediately reminded of Paul's analogy of the Church in his letter to the church at Corinth. He affirms that each one of us occupies and fulfils a unique and indispensable role!

> *"For as the body is one, and hath many members, and all the members of that one body being many are one body so also is Christ."*
>
> (1 Corinthians 12:12, KJV)

> *"For in fact the body is not one member, but many."*
>
> (1 Corinthians. 12:14, NKJV)

"But the manifestation of the spirit is given to everyman to profit withal."

(1 Corinthians 12:7, KJV)

One other important thing about this group was that most of them were what we call laymen. Nonetheless, their deep commitment as believers was never in doubt. They were not just content with merely having a personal faith in Jesus. Nor were they simply satisfied with the practise of their faith that was limited to their homes and church buildings as most Christians today.

They wanted to devote their energies and resources for the welfare of humanity. This, to me, is authentic, New Testament Christianity. I do hope 21st century Christians in Britain, all over Europe, Africa (particularly Nigeria, my place of birth), can read about this group, be inspired and rise up to action.

Today, the Clapham sect is mostly remembered or best known for championing the abolition of the slave trade. However, research has shown that what brought this group together was a lot wider and larger than the issue of the slave trade.

Again Dr Clifford Hill captures the vision that brought this group together when he writes,

"They had a shared faith in God and a shared commitment to the application of their Christian faith to the reformation of society, to improving the living and working conditions of the poor, and above all, to Christian education both at home and overseas. Their shared passion was to get the gospel and teaching of Jesus known throughout the world."[37]

37   *The Wilberforce Connection*, Dr Clifford-Hill, p 50, Monarch Books, 2004

Making History

1. Achieving a vision requires associating with people with common goals. Which groups do you belong to and what is their vision for the community?

2. In reaching out to your community, resources and finances are needed. Do you possess the capacity and skill to network individuals and organizations towards supporting a cause?

3. Making a difference in your community requires either some teamwork or starting off alone and building a followership thereon. Are you a team player or do you like to go 'solo'?

12 *JOHN HOWARD* *Social reformer*

||||||||||||||||||||||||||||| |||||||||||||||||||||||||||||||||||||||||||||||||||||||||||||||||||||||||||||||||||

"To be a success, people need a winning belief system...
I'm going to give it the label 'God'."

Peter Lowe (born 17 June 1938),
British Constructivism artist

"What seems nasty, painful, evil, can become a source
of beauty, joy, and strength, if faced with an open mind.
Every moment is a golden one for him who has the
vision to recognize it as such."

Henry Valentine Miller (1891-1980)

When it comes to social reform, modern Britain owes a great debt to the evangelical revival of the 18th century. The effects of the Wesleyan revival upon the nation were so much that it will take volumes of books to properly document them! Not only did the revivals produce great reformers, but also the fruit of their reforms still resonates today!

John Howard – The Prison Reformer

A classic example of this impact was on Britain's prison system. It was through awakened men that the British prisons became drastically reformed! The revival itself preached the '**fatherhood of God and the brotherhood of all**'. This message led to the same spiritual value being placed upon all persons. As a result, changes were sought for the inhuman conditions that characterised the prison system at that time.

John Howard has been described as one of the most heroic of the 18th century products of the revival. A zealous disciple of John Wesley, it was to this practical Christian's credit that he challenged the emerging social conscience to make sanitary, humane and redemptive prison conditions a matter of public concern. So great was John Howard's appeal to the soul of the British people that "his was the very first statue to be admitted to St. Paul's Cathedral"; and it was raised by public subscription.[38]

Prior to the reform championed by Howard, prison conditions (aptly described as conditions of living death) were far removed from the eyes of the public. In particular, such conditions were unknown to those who were meant to be informed concerning such conditions.

For about seventeen years of his life, Howard gave his time, talents, means and all to champion prison reform. Often waking up around 3am he would travel the length and breadth of Britain and many European nations for the prisoners' cause. During his investigations, he made astonishing discoveries. Many inmates in English prisons included those who had been languishing in cells for months without trial. There were also those awaiting acquittal and others, their persecutors, in order to close their respective cases.

So, what were some of Howard's practical contributions to prison reform? First, as a direct result of his labours, different reforming acts were placed on the statute book. This, to me, is a laudable achievement with the potency of inspiring a rising generation.

"For who hath despised the day of small things?"
(Zechariah 4:10, KJV)

---

38   *England Before and After Wesley,* J. Wesley Bready, p 366

Never despise the days of little beginnings. Never disdain the contribution you can make to your nation. One with God is in the majority. Soldiers of the cross, as I studied the achievements and contributions to prison reforms, almost all the hairs on my head seemed to tingle! Something within me keeps saying, "It can be done again!" I am referring to change agents in the persons of politicians, businessmen and women, who can positively impact our society. May God stir up the likes of John Howard in my generation!

Apart from the above, many decently-built prisons were designed to take the place of previous dungeons. It is because of Howard's contribution to prison reform that he has been rightly referred to as "the father of all modern prison reform". Little wonder then that for his "humanity and zeal"[39], he received the official thanks of the House of Commons.

Making History

1. Visitation to prisons brings us face to face with freedoms we enjoy. Do you believe there is more to be done in present times?

2. Advocacy demands a sense of responsibility to improve the lot of fellow human beings. Do you believe you possess such a gift?

3. Do you think your input cannot be felt or heard? It takes just one step. Are you ready to make that step?

---

39   Ibid, p 368

13 *ELIZABETH FRY*
The prison reformer

"What lies behind us and what lies before us are tiny matters compared to what lies within us."

Ralph Waldo Emerson (1803-1882),
American essayist, lecturer and poet

"Obstacles cannot crush me. Every obstacle yields to stern resolve. He who is fixed to a star does not change his mind."

Leonardo da Vinci (1452-1519),
Italian Renaissance painter, sculptor and architect

Elizabeth Fry has been rightly described as the real successor of John Howard. Born into the Quaker family, her teen years were defined by what Quakers refer to as a 'seeker'; she became one of such.

Under the spiritual influence of the American Quaker preacher, William Slavery, she was deeply touched by the Gospel. The impact was so intense that for the first time,

"she realised there was a God and that Jesus had died to save her."[40]

---

40   *70 Great Christians*, Geoffrey Hanks, page 224, Christian Focus Publications, 2003

In Christian terms, she became a believer or a Christian.

An important incident that would direct and map out the course of her life was when, at a Quaker meeting, it was prophesied of her that she was to be "a light to the blind, speech to the dumb and feet to the lame".[41]

I believe there is a great lesson that all believers must learn from this incidence in the life of Elizabeth Fry. There are too many Christians who limit God's calling or definition of ministry to the four corners of the church. It is not meant to be so. Just as God can and does call people into the pulpit ministry, I believe that God does and is calling many today as reformers whose ministry scope will extend beyond the confines of a church building.

Elizabeth Fry's prison reform started around 1813, when she was introduced to Newgate, London. It has been described as the most notorious prison in the realm. So appalling were prison conditions Elizabeth Fry met that over three hundred women and children were allowed to crowd themselves into four rooms. Here, they did everything, often mixing with male prisoners. In this pathetic state, gambling, drinking, fighting and many other vices became the order of the day. Due to these terrible conditions, Elizabeth Fry began to visit the inmates regularly, from London to as far as Scotland.

One of her enduring habits was to read the Bible and pray with the inmates every day. Often they would listen to her preach. So powerful was her preaching that, '...*the hardest and most impervious criminals melted into reverence and love*'.[42]

Part of her enduring legacy was her establishment of prison schools which taught the women diverse skills, including knitting and sewing. The impact to the women's' self-worth led to the setting up of Ladies' Committees around the country. The primary purpose was to provide support in other prisons.

----

41   Ibid, p 224
42   Ibid, p 370

So successful was Elizabeth Fry's prison reform endeavours that she was invited in 1818 to give evidence of conditions in the state of prisons before a House of Commons Select Committee, and then before the House of Lords.

Furthermore, she campaigned repeatedly against the inhuman and terrible system of transportation that took prisoners from Newgate to Australia. Again, the government often responded to her complaints favourably.

So powerful and impacting was the manifestation of Christian grace from the life of this beautiful Christian woman that an American visitor remarked,

> *"I have seen the greatest wonder in England, I have seen Elizabeth Fry in Newgate, and I have witnessed there the miraculous effects of true Christianity upon the most depraved of human beings."[43]*

At this point, it is important to make a number of observations.

First, in an age where there is much debate about the leadership role of women in the Church, I believe there's a lot to learn from the life of Elizabeth Fry. I strongly believe her life should be a challenge to the Christian women for them to rise up to their full Christian potential in Christ. I also believe God still uses women in significant ways in His kingdom.

Women, if the impact of Elizabeth Fry's life could be felt across this nation, why do you think your own life cannot count for God?

Again let everyone take note. We owe the reforms in our prison system to phenomenal change agents who were radically transformed by the gospel of Jesus Christ!

What we are now building upon and (I dare say) reaping from in these present times are the result of the efforts of Christians of this island. Let every prison inmate across all of

43   *England Before and After Wesley*, W.J. Beady, p 370

Great Britain give thanks to God that people such as John Howard and Elizabeth Fry ever emerged. Their relentless pursuit of improved prison conditions defined what we have today in our prison system.

Making History

1. Do you believe women have a particular role to play in transforming society? If yes, how are supporting your claim?
2. As a woman, do you feel bold or intimidated to speak out against any perceived wrong in society?
3. A change agent is a leader of sorts. Do you possess leadership skill sets that are relevant in social advocacy?

14 *WILLIAM BOOTH The poor man's champion*

> *"No matter what I say, what I believe, and what I do, I'm bankrupt without love."*
>
> (I Corinthians 13:3b)

The Message

> *"Love means living the way God commanded us to live. As you have heard from the beginning, his command is this; live a life of love."*
>
> (2 John 2:6, New Century Version)

The message of Jesus Christ, as preached and practised by the early Church, was primarily biased towards the poor, the marginalized and the socially disadvantaged. Our faith would be incomplete according to Scripture if we see people destitute of daily food and the necessities of life, yet we do not reach out to them in a practical manner (James 2:14-19).

It was the Hebrew prophet who declared,

> *"Loose the bands of wickedness, undo the heavy burdens; let the oppressed go free, break every yoke, deal thy bread to the hungry, bring the poor that are*

cast out to thy house. When thou seest the naked
cover him and hide not thyself from thine own flesh.
Draw out thy soul to the hungry – they that be of thee
shall build the old waste places and thou shalt raise
up the foundations of many generations."

(Isaiah 58:12, KJV)

The above scripture summarises what the Salvation Army
and William Booth stood for. In order to reach the 'hopeless',
William Booth (the founder of the 'Army'), created the East
London Revival Society in 1864. In 1878 this society was
re-organised and christened the Salvation Army.

So what were the prevalent conditions before the birth of
the Salvation Army?

General Booth in his work, *The Darkest England and The*
Way Out, has given us a picture of England in the 19th century.
He writes,

> *'Darkest England may be described as consisting broadly*
> *of three circles, one within the other. The outer and*
> *widest circle is inhabited by the starving and homeless,*
> *but honest, poor. The second by those who live by vice;*
> *and the third and innermost region at the centre is*
> *peopled by those who exist by crime.'*[44]

Just as today, there existed a class gulf between the rich and
poor during the 19th century. Although this social problem
was rampant throughout the nation, yet nowhere was it more
pronounced than in the East End of London. There was much
poverty and misery in this particular region. According to
Geoffrey Hanks, at the second half of the century, there were an
estimated five hundred philanthropic agencies at work in the

---

44   *The Darkest England and The Way Out,* General Booth, p 25, International
      Headquarters of the Salvation Army, London, 1890

East End of London. They were spending about £3.5 million in charity, yet could not stem the tide of poverty.[45]

During this period, the bulk of the Church made little or no attempt to minister to the poor and the downtrodden in society. It was left to the Salvation Army to champion the cause of the poor, first in the East End of London then across the nation and thereafter to several nations of the world.

We may not appreciate today the social reformation that William Booth championed. These reforms transformed many lives in our nation. A mental grip of the bleak conditions which pervaded then will give a clear picture of how terrible things were for the poor. In those days, it was a common phenomenon for people to die of hunger because they were unemployed and, as such, unable to afford a meal.

General Booth shares the pathetic case of such a person in his book,

> *"Last year, a man whose name was never known was walking through St. James Park when three of our shelter men saw him suddenly fall. They thought he was drunk, but found he had fainted. They carried him to the bridge and gave him to the police. They took him to St. George's hospital where he died. It appeared that he had, according to his own tale, walked up from Liverpool, and had been without food for five days. The doctor, however, said he had gone longer than that. The jury returned a verdict of 'Death from Starvation'."*[46]

At that time, the main body of the Christian Church made little or no attempt to evangelise the poor and the down-and-outs. It was the radical approach of the Salvation Army that made the gospel meaningful to the thousands of these individuals.

45 *70 Great Christians*, Geoffrey Hanks
46 *In Darkest England And The Way Out*, General Booth, International Head-
    quarters, Salvation Army, London, 1890

J. Wesley Bready has summarised the scope and the achievements of the Salvation Army in his work 'England Before and After Wesley', when he wrote,

> "Besides all its moral and spiritual teaching facilities, the Salvation Army conducts an amazing retinue of social services. Its hostels and shelters provide scores of thousands of free beds for the homeless and forlorn. Millions of free meals are annually given to the hungry, through its kitchens and canteens. Employment is found for large numbers out of work. As for criminals, prisoners, and their dependents, the 'Army' annually assists many thousands of these with tenderness and an understanding no state institution could emulate. It provides many companies of trained nurses and midwives, in quarters where their services are a 'God-send'. It runs maternity homes, hospitals, crèches, industrial homes, 'eventide homes', seaside camps, land colonies, migration centres, slum sisterhoods, prison visitation corps and most winsome rescue homes for unmarried mothers. For uncompromising as is their morality, never do Salvationists look upon young unmarried mothers as prostitutes."[47]

No doubt, William Booth will be regarded as one of the great men that made Great Britain great. Let it also be noted that the accomplishments of William Booth were because he was a changed man, changed because of the Gospel of Jesus Christ.

So what would we regard as some of the most important contributions of William Booth to this nation?

First William Booth went for the dregs of society, the lowest, the poorest and the most abused. These were the people he gave priority to at the expense of those who were rich and

47   Ibid, p 414

admired. It must be pointed out that all these happened in an age when the established Church did not want to be disturbed by the persistent needs of the poor and downtrodden. So successful was Booth that in his days he reached several thousand people every month.

Secondly, William Booth was also involved in social campaigns. A classic example was his campaign for the Age of Consent, which was then twelve but was later raised to fourteen and then to sixteen. It must be pointed out that this was a time when many people thought this should not be the domain of the Church.

Furthermore, William Booth managed to combine the spiritual and the social Gospel. Up till then most churches concentrated either on one or the other. William Booth always held the two together, the Social and spiritual Gospel. He strongly believed one cannot listen with an empty stomach to someone preaching.

On the role of women, William Booth and the Salvation Army were the first Christian organisation to place women on the same level with men. It must be noted that the Victorian Age was basically patriarchal.

Finally at a time when people were thinking of Darkest Africa, it was William Booth who pointed to Darkest England, referring to the plight of the poor and the socially marginalized.

Making History

1. Compassion is a key Christian virtue for reaching out to the poor. Do you make time to minister to the poor in your neighbourhood?

2. What vision is there in reaching out to the poor in your community?

3. What is your personal motto for rendering assistance for those in need?

4. Why not raise the issue of the poor's pathetic plight in your community at the next Board, deacons', elders' or church meeting?

THE SPHERE
OF RELIGION

15 DAVID LIVINGSTONE
Missionary statesman

"I place no value on anything I have or may possess, except in relation to the kingdom of Christ. If anything will advance the interest of the kingdom, it shall be given away or kept, only as by giving or keeping it I shall promote the glory of Him to whom I owe all my hopes in time and eternity."[48]

"People talk of the sacrifice I have made in spending so much of my life in Africa. Can that be called a sacrifice which is simply paid back as a small part of a great debt owing to our God, which we can never repay? Is that a sacrifice which brings its own blest reward in healthful activity, the consciousness of doing good, peace of mind, and a bright hope of a glorious destiny hereafter? Away with the word in such a view and with such a thought! It is emphatically no sacrifice, say rather it is a privilege. Anxiety, sickness, suffering, or danger now and then with a foregoing of common conveniences and charities of this life may make us pause and cause the spirit to waver and the soul to sink, but let this only be for a moment. All these are nothing when compared with the glory which shall be revealed in and for us. I never made a sacrifice."[49]

48   www.wikipedia/wiki/david_livingstone /legacy
49   wikiquote.org/wiki/david_livingstone

Without doubt, David Livingstone stands out as one of the most popular national heroes of the late 19th century in Victorian Britain. In British history, he is hailed and remembered as a first-class Protestant missionary and much more; a scientific investigator, explorer, and an advocate for commercial empire!

He was born on the 19th of March 1813 to a working class family in Blantyre, Scotland. The second of seven children, he was raised in very humble surroundings.

Like many history-makers, Livingstone had an unquenchable desire for education right from his childhood. This he acquired at great price. He was taught to read and write by his father.

Despite working fourteen hours a day from the age of ten, Livingstone still enrolled for evening classes provided by the company. His passion to acquire knowledge and be educated was intense. He bought a Latin grammar book with his first week's pay, a lesson for all would-be world changers.

David Livingstone survived his difficult years of schooling by snatching glances at a book propped up on his spinning jenny and poring over homework assignments until midnight. At the age of 19 he was promoted. With his increased wages by 1836 he had saved enough money to gain admission into Anderson's University, Glasgow to study medicine. There he studied under Andrew Buchanan, MD.

In 1840 he moved to London to complete his medical studies at the British and Foreign Medical School, the Aldersgate Street Dispensary, Charing Cross Hospital and Moorfield Hospital. At the end of the year, he qualified as a Licentiate of the Faculty of Physicians and Surgeons of Glasgow.

Regarding his religious background, Livingstone grew up in a pious church-going family who had left the established Anglican Church to attend an independent chapel. After his conversion, Livingstone dreamt of becoming a missionary doctor to China. This dream, however, was cut short by international political friction between Britain and China. This strain eventually led to the opium war.

His choice of Africa as missionary destination was greatly influenced by Robert Moffat. This veteran six-foot tall missionary to Africa and his mentor would later become his father-in-law!

Mr. Moffat continually teased his missionary protégé with missionary possibilities. He would tell him thrilling stories and opportunities for evangelism beyond Kuruman in "the vast place to the North" where he had "sometimes seen, in the morning sun, the smoke of a thousand villages, where no missionary had ever been".[50]

As a pioneer, like Paul of old, Livingstone became convinced of his mission to reach new people in the interior of Africa and introduce them to Christianity, as well as freeing them from slavery. These burning convictions inspired his explorations.

From 1841 to when he died in 1873, David Livingstone gave himself to the exploration of Central and Southern Africa. Initially, his aims were to spread Christianity and bring commerce and civilization to these regions. However, his subsequent missions were centred more on exploration, first of the Zambezi River and its tributaries and later to find the source of the Nile River.

So, what were some of the specific contributions and lasting legacies that David Livingstone made?

Livingstone was one of the first Europeans to make a transcontinental journey across Africa, from Luansa on the Atlantic to Quelimare on the Indian Ocean near the mouth of the Zambezi. This was between 1854 and 1856. Despite repeated attempts by Europeans (especially by the Portuguese), Central and Southern Africa had not been successfully crossed by Europeans at that latitude. This was because of their susceptibility to malaria, dysentery and sleeping sickness. These ailments were common in the interior.

To this day in Britain and much of the Commonwealth (and the world at large) the abolition of the slave trade

---

50   *From Jerusalem to Irian Jaya*, Ruth A. Tucker, p 156, Zondervan, Michigan, 2004

is mostly associated with William Wilberforce. However, Wilberforce does not stand alone in bringing about the end of slave traffic in Africa. David Livingstone's letters, books and journals did a lot to stir up public support for the abolition of slavery. In a letter to the editor of the *New York Herald*, Livingstone writes,

> *"And if my disclosure regarding the terrible Ujijan slavery should lead to the suppression of the East Coast slave trade, I shall regard that as a greater matter by far than the discovery of all the Nile sources together."*[51]

On the missionary front, Livingstone was not as successful as his exploratory pursuits. New mission societies were formed as a result of his many strategic and high profile speaking engagements around the country. Another factor that led to the founding of mission societies was the documentation of his missionary chronicles in his book, *Missionary Travels and Researches in South-Africa*. A classic example was the Universities Mission to Central Africa (UMCA). Just as the death of martyrs had always been a seed for the growth of the Church, the death of David Livingstone also had a tremendous positive impact on missionary fervour and passion.

On the impact his death had on missionary activities, Ruth Tucker, in *From Jerusalem to Irian Jaya*, remarks:

> *"The death of David Livingstone had a tremendous psychological impact on the English speaking world. Missionary fervour reached a high pitch as zealous young men and women volunteered for overseas duty, no matter what the cost."*[52]

51 Wikipedia
52 *From Jerusalem to Irian Jaya*, Ruth A. Tucker, p 163, Zondervan, Michigan, 2004

David Livingstone was not only a pioneer missionary and explorer, but he was also a great campaigner for commerce. He saw nothing wrong or incompatible between Christianity and commerce. He further believed that the solution to the illegitimate slave trade was to bring legitimate commerce to Africa by way of a navigable trade.

On the 1st of May 1873, David Livingstone's servant found his "master" kneeling, as if in prayer, by the side of his bed. His body was stretched forward, his head buried in his hands upon the pillows, dead!

His faithful servants, Susi and Chuma, thought that there was no better way to pay their respects than to deliver his body and personal papers to his former associates at the coast. After burying his heart under a Mpundu tree, his body was dried in the sun until it was mummified and then carried over land fifteen hundred miles to the coast. In England, Livingstone was given a state funeral at Westminster Abbey. It was attended by dignitaries from all over the country.

It is to his enduring legacy and unparalleled achievements that David Livingstone was buried in Westminster Abbey, reserved for royals and those who have contributed in no small measure to the greatness of our nation.

The location of his grave is at the centre of the nave. The inscription on the stone is in brass, which I have been privileged many times to personally read:

"BROUGHT BY FAITHFUL HANDS OVER LAND AND SEA HERE RESTS
DAVID LIVINGSTONE, MISSIONARY, TRAVELLER, PHILANTROPIST,
BORN MARCH 19, 1813 AT BLANTYRE, LANARKSHIRE, DIED MAY 1
1873 AT CHITAMBO'S VILLAGE, ULALA. FOR 30 YEARS HIS LIFE
WAS SPENT IN AN UNWEARIED EFFORT TO EVANGELISE THE NATIVE
RACES, TO EXPLORE THE UNDISCOVERED SECRETS, TO ABOLISH
THE DESOLATING SLAVE TRADE OF CENTRAL AFRICA, WHERE WITH
HIS LAST WORDS HE WROTE, "ALL I CAN ADD IN MY SOLITUDE, MAY

HEAVEN'S RICH BLESSING COME DOWN ON EVERY ONE, AMERICA, ENGLISH, OR TURK, WHO WILL HELP TO HEAL THIS OPEN SORE OF THE WORLD."

Making History

1. 'Knowledge is Power' as the saying goes. How much of it do you expose yourself to on a regular basis?

2. How much of your resources do you commit to building up your knowledge base?

3. What inspires you the most and what are you willing to deny yourself in order to achieve it?

4. What lessons can you learn from the life of David Livingstone and how do you intend to incorporate them into your life and ministry?

16 *CHARLES HADDON SPURGEON*
The prince of preachers

||||||||||||||||||||||||||||| |||||||||||||||||||||||||||||||||||||||||||||||||||||||||||||||||||||||||||

*"C. H. Spurgeon was to Nineteenth century England
what D. L. Moody was to America."*

William Young Fullerton (1857-1932),
Baptist preacher, administrator and writer

*"For the earnest expectation of creation eagerly waits
for the revealing of the sons of God."*

(Romans 8:19, NKJV)

At 21, Charles Spurgeon was already the most popular
preacher in London. For many years he preached to crowds
of about ten thousand souls at the Exeter Hall and the Surrey
Music Hall. Later on, when the Metropolitan Tabernacle was
built, several thousand gathered every Sunday to listen to the
Prince of Preachers, as he was then called. One can appreciate
the impact that he made on London if we remember that
almost one hundred and fifty years after being laid to rest
average church attendance in the UK today is not more than
a hundred souls. Even up till now, no single church in Britain
has been able to surpass the number of people that attended
his weekly meetings.

Charles Spurgeon was born on the 19th of June 1834, in Kelvedon Essex in England. He was from a generation of preachers, converted to Christianity on the 6th of January 1850 at the age of 16. On his way to a scheduled appointment, a snow storm forced him to cut short his intended journey. He had to take refuge in a seemingly primitive Methodist Chapel in Colchester where he heard the Gospel preached from Isaiah 45:22 (KJV),

> "Look unto me, and be ye saved, all the ends of the earth, for I am God, and there is none else."

Later, on the 4th of April the same year, he was admitted to the church at Newmarket.

In 1856 he married Susannah Thompson. Their twin sons, Thomas and Charles, were born on the 20th of September 1857.

Spurgeon's preaching ministry started in Teversham in 1850 at the age of fifteen. The next year he accepted his first pastorate at the Baptist Chapel in Water Beach. The church quickly grew from fewer than a dozen congregants to more than four hundred. This growth spread Spurgeon's reputation as a heavily anointed preacher. It caught the attention of New Park Street, London's largest Baptist Church. He was invited to preach there in December 1853, and following a brief probationary period, he agreed to move to London and become the church's new pastor. Thus began the ministry of one of God's greatest generals of all times.

The Best Preacher of His Day!

Without doubt, among the company of preachers of the 19th century in London, Charles Spurgeon was *primus inter pares*! By the age of 22, just about 6 years after his conversion,

Spurgeon was the most popular preacher of the day. For most of his pastorate, he preached to over 10,000 souls, a forerunner of what one can call in the modern parlance a "mega–church". This scenario was unknown in his day, a feat unparalleled in 21st century Britain. So popular was Spurgeon's ministry in the 19th century that if you wanted to hear him preach, you had to be seated for at least 30 minutes before the service started, an exploit that many God fearing Christians are praying be repeated in our days!

Walter Thornbury, in "*Old and New London*" (1897), once described one such meeting at Surrey.

> "*A congregation consisting of 10,000 souls streaming into the hall, mounting the galleries, humming, buzzing, and swarming – like a mighty hive of bees – eager to secure at first the best places, and at least, any place at all, after waiting more than half an hour. For if you wish to have a seat, you must be there at least that space of time in advance. Mr Spurgeon ascended his tribune to the hum, and rush, and trampling of men, succeeded a low, concentrated thrill and murmur of devotion, which seemed to run at once, like an electric current, through the breast of everyone present, and by this magnetic chain the preacher held us fast bound for about two hours. It is not my purpose to give a summary of his discourse. It is enough to say of his voice, that its power and volume are sufficient to reach everyone in that vast assembly of his language, that it is neither high-flown nor homely, of his style, that it is at times familiar at times declamatory, but always happy, and often eloquent of his doctrine, that neither the "Calvinist nor the 'Baptist' appears in the forefront of the battle which is waged by Mr Spurgeon with relentless animosity. And with Gospel weapon against religion, hypocrisy, pride, and those secret bosom sins which so easily beset*

a man in daily life, and to sum up all in a word, it is
enough to say, of the man himself, that he impresses
you with a perfect conviction of his sincerity"[53]

At the height of his ministry, Spurgeon preached at the fast day, 7th of October 1857, to the largest crowd ever, 23,654 people. This was at The Crystal Palace in London.[54]

Spurgeon's Sermons

One of the most enduring legacies that Charles Spurgeon left behind was his sermons. It was his custom to write out all his sermons before he preached, but would eventually approach the pulpit with an outline sketch.

Stenographers would take down the sermon as it was delivered and Spurgeon would then have opportunity to make revisions to the transcripts the following day for immediate publication. It was further said that his weekly sermon was sold for a penny each, widely circulated all around London and beyond. These sermons are still preserved today and without any controversy they remain one of the all time bestselling series of writings ever published in history.[55]

Charles Spurgeon was a prolific author of many types of works including sermons, an autobiography, commentaries, and books on prayer, devotionals, magazines, poetry, hymns and many more. By the time of his death, he had preached nearly 3,600 sermons and published 49 volumes of commentaries, sayings, anecdotes, illustrations and devotions. Most of these works are available in wide circulation around the globe, through Spurgeonline. Today Spurgeon's works have

53   Wikipedia.org/wiki/Charles_Spurgeon
54   Wikipedia
55   Wikipedia

been translated into over twenty languages including Arabic, Spanish and Tamil.

Spurgeon in History

The question then arises: did Charles Haddon Spurgeon make any mark on history? How well did he place his footprints on the sands of time? How enduring has been the labour of the 'Prince of Preachers'?

To Spurgeon himself, the real impact of his work would be felt long after he died. He once remarked:

> *"I sometimes think if I were in heaven I should almost wish to visit my work at the tabernacle to see whether it will abide the test of time and prosper when I am gone...."[56]*

Spurgeon's College (1857)

> *"'...My first-born and best beloved' this is my life's work, to which I believe God has called me, therefore; I must do it."*
>
> *Spurgeon speaking about his college*

The greatness of a man is not only measured by his achievements during his lifetime, but by his enduring legacy. How many people did such a man impact and empower? How long did his work last after his demise? How far-reaching was his influence, even beyond his own geographical borders?

Judging by the above criteria, Charles Haddon Spurgeon excelled gallantly, without a shadow of doubt.

56   *The Forgotten Spurgeon*, Iain Murray, p 258

One of the most enduring legacies that he bequeathed to Europe as a whole (and Britain in particular) is the Pastors' College. The institution is now called Spurgeon's College and is situated in South Norwood, London.

Spurgeon placed a very high premium on the training of would-be preachers as young as twenty three years old. He devoted a large portion of his means to such service. At one time, when the college was low on funding, Spurgeon offered to sell his carriage and horses to sustain the school.

Again, on the importance that Charles Spurgeon placed on ministerial training, W. Y. Fullerton writes in his monumental work, Charles Haddon Spurgeon: A Biography,

> "It was said of him at the time, "He is not by any means the foe of learning, but he is more the friend of souls of men that he sought by word and example to instil into his disciples. He said to his own students often what once he said to those at Cheshunt College; "You are preparing for the ministry, but do not wait till you have entered it – you may never live to do that. Win your highest honour, secure your best diploma now. Begin with speed, with fire, with learning and live to save men now."[57]

So successful has been the college that by 1886 it had a third of the students in the nine Baptist colleges in the kingdom and a third of the income.

At his death in 1892, nearly nine hundred men had been trained for the ministry. Soon, students began to come from all across the United Kingdom. One student was said to have walked all the way from the Highlands of Scotland.[58]

Today, students have been trained from all parts of the world and their mission is practically in every nation!

57   *The Spurgeon's Archive*, www.spurgeon.org/misc/bio.htm
58   W. Y. Fullerton, www.reforedreader.org/rbb/spurgeon

It should be mentioned that during Spurgeon's early ministry days the institution's influence was international. Graduates were sent to Australia, New Zealand, Canada, Amsterdam, Haiti, the Falkland Islands, South America, South Africa, Spain, Italy, India, China, and Japan. Spurgeon never ventured beyond Continental Europe. However, through his college and the graduates, he exerted an influence beyond the borders of Great Britain.

Spurgeon's Social Endeavours

"Then Jesus answered and said, " A certain man went down from Jerusalem to Jericho and fell among thieves, who stripped him of his clothing, wounded him, and departed, leaving him half dead. Now by chance a certain priest came down that road. And when he saw him, he passed by on the other side. Likewise a Levite, when he arrived at the place, came and looked, and passed by on the other side. But a certain Samaritan, as he journeyed, came where he was. And when he saw him, he had compassion. So he went to him and bandaged his wounds. Pouring on oil and wine, he set him on his own animal, brought him to an inn, and took care of him. On the next day, when he departed, he took out two denarii, gave them to the inn keeper and said to him, "Take care of him, and whatever you spend, when I come again, I will repay you." So which of these three do you think was neighbour to him who fell among the thieves?"

(Luke 10:30-36, NKJV)

"What does it profit, my brethren, if someone says he has faith but does not have works? Can faith save

him? If a brother or sister is naked and destitute of daily food, and one of you says to them, "Depart in peace, be warmed and filled" but you do not give the things which are needed for the body, what does it profit? Thus, also faith by itself, if it does not have works, is dead."

(James 2:14-17, NKJV)

"Pure and undefiled religion before God and the father is this – to visit the orphans and widows in their trouble, and to keep oneself unspotted from the world."

(James 1:27, NKJV)

Charles Spurgeon was not only a man totally given over to preaching and training, but also to extensive social endeavours. Like his Master from Nazareth, he not only preached to the multitudes but also catered for their practical and daily needs by feeding them. Spurgeon's holistic ministry to the orphans, street children and socially disadvantaged is a legacy. This legacy has not only outlived him, but is still very much alive today.

Spurgeon, over his lifetime, was involved in several social projects. However, his work with orphanages stands out. Several hundred children who otherwise would have roamed the streets as thieves and vagrants were housed, fed and trained in the Word of God. Spurgeon was reported to have once remarked,

"We are a large church and we must have a large heart for this city."[59]

At another time, he remarked,

---

59   *A Baptist Page Portrait*, Charles H. Spurgeon, www.wholesomewords.org/biography/biospurgeon

> *"The God that answers by orphanages, let HIM*
> *be Lord."[60]*

Again W. Y. Fuller, from his monumental work, comments on the significance of Spurgeon's ministry to the orphans:

> *"The orphanage is the greatest sermon Mr Spurgeon*
> *ever preached."*

Today, well after 150 years, Spurgeon's child care operations continue but in another form.

In 1879 the orphanage was closed. Spurgeon then moved into community-based work with families. He developed a wide range of services which were delivered through over 90 projects across the UK and are still running today. In over half of these, they work in partnership with local churches.

Over the last decade Spurgeon's Ministries have developed significant work overseas, particularly in Eastern Europe, but also in Africa and Mexico.

Charles Spurgeon – A Defender of Orthodoxy!

One of the most enduring legacies that I believe Charles Spurgeon has left for the coming generation is that he was a defender of the Faith. In present times, liberalism has crept into the Church of Jesus Christ. At a time when the preachers of the day are expected to wield their sword and fight for the truth, they follow popular opinion. Spurgeon was not a preacher who would compromise the infallibility of God's Word.

We are charged in God's Holy Word to defend the faith:

---

60   W. Y. Fullerton, www.reforedreader.org/rbb/spurgeon

"Beloved, while I was very diligent to write to you concerning our common salvation, I found it necessary to write to you exhorting you to contend earnestly for the faith which was once for all delivered to the saints"

(Jude 1:3, NKJV)

Towards the end of Spurgeon's life, there seemed to be a steady decline among evangelicals, particularly through the influence of liberalism.

Spurgeon responded by publishing articles in his magazine, *The Sword and Trowel*, to expose the cancerous liberal doctrine eating deep into the Church. This was later known as the downgrade controversy. On the problem, C. H. Spurgeon wrote,

"The time has come for Christians to stir; the house is being robbed, its very walls are being digged down, but the good people who are in the bed are too fond of the warmth, and too much afraid of getting broken heads, to go downstairs and meet the burglars... Inspiration and speculation cannot long abide in peace. Compromise there can be none. We cannot hold the inspiration of the word, and yet reject it, we cannot believe in the atonement and deny it, we cannot talk of the doctrine of the fall and yet talk of the evolution of spiritual life from human nature...One way or another we must go. Decision is the virtue of the hair."[61]

I really find Spurgeon very inspirational. All 21st century preachers must not only read about Spurgeon, but they must follow in his footsteps. In an age where pastors are more concerned to be more politically correct than be Biblically

61   *A Baptist Page Portrait*, C. H. Spurgeon, www.wholesomewords,org/biography/biospurgeon

correct, needed at this hour are Ministry Teams; Pastors, Prophets, Evangelists, who will raise up the standard. The need is even more urgent as the blessed and consecrated name of our Lord is been desecrated by a decadent generation.

Perhaps the best way to summarise Spurgeon's legacy would be to quote his funeral eulogy by Heber Evans, who summed up his legacy thus,

> *"But there is one Charles Haddon Spurgeon whom we cannot bury; there is not earth enough in Norwood to bury him – The Spurgeon of History."*[62]

Again, one week after Spurgeon's home going, B. H. Carroll preached an entire sermon on his larger influence around the world. He remarked,

> *"Yes, Spurgeon is dead. The tallest and broadest oak in the forest of time is fallen. The sweetest, most silvery and far-reaching voice that published the glad tidings since apostolic times is hushed. The hand whose sickle cut the widest swathe in the ripened grain fields of redemption lies folded and nerveless on a pulseless breast, whose heart when beating kept time with every human joy and woe. But he was ready to be offered. He fought a good fight. He kept the faith, and while we weep, he wears the triple crown of life and joy and glory, which God, the righteous judge has conferred upon him... In answer to the question; How do you account for Spurgeon? The answer is... God"*[63]

62   *A Baptist Page Portrait*, www.wholesomewords.org
63   wholesomewords.org

Making History

1. Preaching the Word of God requires a hunger for things of the Spirit. How often do you study the Bible?

2. Can you identify 3 ways in which the life of Charles Spurgeon has inspired you?

3. Making a difference through the Gospel includes speaking out against perceived wrongs in the society. Are you a voice in your community or neighbourhood?

17 *JOHN WESLEY The Revivalist and national transformer*

||||||||||||||||||||||||||||| |||||||||||||||||||||||||||||||||||||||||||||||||||||||||||||||||||||||||||||||||||||

"I say to you today, my friends, that in spite of the difficulties and frustrations of the moment, I still have a dream."

Dr. Martin Luther King Jr.,
American civil rights activist and clergyman

"God has given each of you some special abilities; be sure to use them to help each other, passing on to others God's many kinds of blessings."

(I Peter 4:10)

The Living Bible

A survey was taken in 2005 by the British Broadcasting Corporation with the question: 'Who was the most influential man in English history?' The BBC reported on the World News that the answer was John Wesley.[64]

Why would they choose a five-foot two, 115-pound man? I believe the answer is not farfetched. First, the Great Awakening

---

64   *The World's Greatest Revivals*, Fred & Sharon Wright, p 129, Destiny Image, USA

that he led in the 18th century had a far-reaching impact which eventually touched every strata of our society and several nations of the earth. Secondly, his legacy is still very much felt around the world in the 21st century.

John Pollock, in his monumental work, *Wesley The Preacher*, summarizes the impact that John Wesley made on society and on the world at large,

> *"John Wesley in a real sense belongs to the whole world and to every age and church. He is particularly relevant to his own country because his revival was a primary factor in changing national attitudes and character. Victorian values (in the true sense of the phrase) are really Wesley values, which are Christian values."*[65]

John Wesley was born in 1703. He was an Anglican clergyman, evangelist and the founder of what is today called the Methodist Church. He was the 15th child of a former non-conformist minister and a graduate of Oxford University. While still at Oxford, he formed a religious club, The Holy Club, with his brother, Charles.

Without doubt, John Wesley was a child of destiny. The hand of God was definitely upon him for miraculous occurrences were part of his life, even from his youth.

There was a fire incident that put his life in danger. 'Jacky', as he was fondly called, had been forgotten by his family in the house where they were staying when the fire became an inferno. However, by divine providence, he would be regarded as "...a brand plucked out of the burning"; he survived the ordeal. After this miraculous escape, the Reverend Samuel Wesley, his house in ashes, his books and writings gone, cried out in joy.

---

65   *Wesley The Preacher*, p 11, Kingsway, Eastbourne, 1989

> *"Come neighbours, let us kneel down let us give thanks to God, He has given me all eight children, let the house go. I am rich enough."*[66]

Two important milestones in Wesley's life are worth mentioning. First was his missionary trip to Georgia, a British Colony in America. This was forty-one years before America gained her independence. Wesley had a frustratingly short missionary journey. Thereafter, he returned home bemoaning the experience.

> *"I went to America to convert the Indians, but oh wretched man that I am, who will convert me?"*

God did not keep him waiting long before He answered his prayers.

The second milestone event was his conversion on Wednesday evening of May the 24th 1738. He had reluctantly gone for a meeting in Aldersgate Street, London. At the meeting, someone was reading Luther's preface to the Epistle to the Romans. John Wesley declares,

> *"At about a quarter before noon, while he was describing the change which God works in the heart through faith in Christ, I felt my heart strangely warmed. I felt I did trust in Christ, Christ alone for salvation, and assurance was given me that He had taken away my sins, even mine, and saved me from the law of sin and death."*

This conversion, coupled with that of both his brother Charles and George Whitefield, would permanently change the spiritual landscape of this country. We can never fully appreciate the

66   Ibid, p 16

contributions or the impact that John Wesley made on our nation except we have a picture of what English society looked like prior to the Great Awakening.

Britain Before The Great Awakening

Conditions before the Great Awakening were in a terribly desperate state. It would not be far from the truth to say that things were at very low ebb.

Moral lapses pervaded the whole of society right from the very top. As it was during the days of some Old Testament monarchs, so was it in England. The decay had set in from the ruling house. The first two Georges of the Royal House of Hanover were not only unfaithful to their wives, but they had regular affairs with several other women.

The Church, which was supposed to be the foundation and pillar of truth, was in such a mess. First, there was a departure from belief in the authority of Scripture. Also, the nature and character of God was attacked. The person of Jesus was declared to be no more than a human being. He was stripped of divinity.

Furthermore, the miraculous and the supernatural were almost totally wiped out of Christianity. Christianity then, as is today, was almost reduced to humanism and philosophical speculations.

Bishop Butler gives an apt description of the state of Christianity in our nation. He asserted,

> *"Christianity was wearing out of the minds of men. It was everywhere being held up to ridicule, and all that it stood for was being made the object of scorn."*[67]

---

67   *The Trumpet Sounds for Great Britain*, Vol 1, David E Gardner, p 63, Christian Foundation Publications, Cheshire UK, 1980

Colin Whitaker further paints another grim picture of what pervaded in those times in his book,

> *"Our whole population seem to be given over to one*
> *form of orgy or the other, particularly drunkenness,*
> *this made the very name of Englishmen to stink in*
> *the nostrils of other nations. Drunk for a penny, dead*
> *drunk for two pence. Straw to lie on was a common*
> *sign outside the pubs of that time. Our theatre was*
> *shockingly vulgar and depraved. Wesley referred to the*
> *obscenity of the stage – that sink of all corruption."[68]*

He summarizes the deplorable situation of things when he writes:

> *"The literature of the period would even today be*
> *classed mostly as "hard porn". Polygamy, fornication,*
> *homosexuality were not considered sinful. Violence*
> *was rampant. Gangs of drunken ruffians paraded the*
> *streets and subjected women to nameless outrages, and*
> *defenceless men to abominable tortures. The constables*
> *shared the drunken habits of the time and were mainly*
> *corrupt. Sport was cruel and brutal, such as bear and*
> *bull baiting and cock fighting. Pugilism was savage and*
> *murderous and even women took part."[69]*

During the early days of the 18th century, England had declined in morality and spirituality to a level almost unparalleled in our history, as described above. We were a nation ripe for divine judgement. This is where I believe we are today; it is either Revival or Judgement.

Rather than Judgement, God gave us a Great Awakening which was to turn things around, and bring about a national

---

68   Great Revivals, Colin Whittaker, p 45, Marshalls, Basingstoke, UK, 1984
69   Ibid, p 45

transformation. This is what I strongly yearn to occur in Britain today.

Wesley's notable ministry came to a close in 1791. By this time, he had served his Master's Kingdom for over 50 years. During this period, he had travelled 250,000 miles and preached 40,000 sermons. In addition, he had also trained about 140,000 practising members as disciples through his sermons. He further mentored some 1,500 travelling preachers who were the instruments of the Great Awakening.

Commenting on the revival, Arnold Dallimore remarks,

"As an evangelical revivalist, he must be considered the greatest since the Apostles."[70]

Why, then, did the survey of the BBC report that John Wesley was the most influential man in English history?

In practical terms, what did he contribute to the greatness of our nation? In what ways, if any, did John Wesley leave a permanent legacy on the sands of time?

Do we owe any debt at all to the father of Methodism? I strongly believe we owe him a lot. It is important to state from the onset that Wesley had a deep conviction about God's purpose for him. He believed firmly that his calling was to open the Word of God for his nation, drawing men and women to God through Christ.

This act, in turn, would reclaim their homes, towns and country from paganism and corruption. Wesley's central understanding of Christianity was that individual redemption leads to social regeneration. Wesley preached and believed that social changes are an inevitable by-product and useful piece of conversion.

First, it must be noted that God used Wesley to fan the flames of the Great Awakening. As a result of the revival, the

70   Ibid, p 53

whole tone of our national life was totally transformed. All facets, areas, and departments were cleansed, compared to earlier descriptions of the appalling conditions prevalent before the Great Awakening.

The national transformation as it was in the 18th century is the most urgent need of our nation today.

Let me yet again echo that it was men and women who received the Gospel of Jesus Christ and became born again that were used to change society. For the real problem (as it was then and is today) is the problem of sin in the heart of men. Once this is dealt with by accepting Jesus Christ and living by the Bible standards, coupled with sufficient numbers of changed men in the society, national transformation is bound to occur.

"Give me a hundred men who fear nothing but God and Hell...," Wesley once remarked, *"...and I will change the world."*

It was men changed by the revival that became leaders and moving forces in many social issues of the day. We owe the abolition of the slave trade to men who had been touched by the revival. They were renewed individuals who preached equality of all men before God. These Christians include William Wilberforce, Zachary Macaulay, Henry Thornton, John Venn and many others who constituted the Clapham Sect.

John Wesley himself was a keen abolitionist, for he spoke out and wrote against the slave trade. He published a pamphlet on slavery titled, *Thoughts Upon Slavery* (1774).

In one of his tracts against slave trade, Wesley once remarked,

> *"Liberty is the right of every human creature, as long as he breathes the vital air, and no human law can deprive him of that right which he derives from the Law of nature."*[71]

---

71   *Thoughts Upon Slavery*, John Wesley; *Holiness of Heart and Life*, Charles/ Vigoyen, 1996, Oct 2009

Again it was through the fruits of the revival that our prison system became more humanised, and the British penal code also became drastically reformed.

John Howard, the *Champion of Prison Reform*, was an evangelical Christian and a product of the revival. He was in fact an ardent disciple of John Wesley.

This social reformer travelled several hundred miles throughout our great country and expended a lot of his personal fortune to make sure that prisoners were not held under inhuman conditions. These conditions were prevalent in those days.

Elizabeth Fry, who followed in the wake of John Howard, was also a product of the revival. Her influence is mostly noted in London's Newgate Prison. Furthermore, it must noted that popular education grew directly out of the evangelical revival. It was out of this revival that the Sunday School movement emerged. It swept across our nation throughout the 18th century and then later on internationally. Furthermore, many learnt to read and write through this Sunday School movement.

On John Wesley's contribution to education of the masses, the Encyclopaedia Britannica states,

> *"No man in the Eighteenth century did so much to create a taste for good reading and to supply it with books at the lowest prices."*[72]

The more I read about the history of this country, particularly the effects of the revival, the more my heart yearns that God will send us another Holy Ghost revival just like the 18th century. This is our great need of today.

David E. Gardner has done an excellent work on the effects of the Great Awakening on our society. On our hospital system he writes:

72   *The Book That Made Your World*, Vishal Mangalwadi, p 267, Tennessee, USA, 2011

"It is to changed men that Britain owes or owed its voluntary hospital system."[73]

Sir George Newman observed that an unprecedented improvement in public health accompanied the progress of the Eighteenth century revival. In addition, it was due to the effect of the revival that the splendid, voluntary hospital facilities of modern England came to be more associated with a spiritual rather than with a materialistic concept of life.

J. W Bready says,

"The British voluntary hospital system, the only major hospital system in the world which was supported almost exclusively by the free-will gifts of any appreciative public was a product of the evangelical revival."[74]

It must be said that Wesley himself opened the first free medical dispensary for the poor and a rheumatism clinic, and he also wrote a treatise on medicine.

Again, the restoration of the Bible's authority in the English world as a consequence of the revival amounted to a civilization finding its soul.

Vishal Mangalwadi remarks,

"Writings of a number of literary men and women give evidence of their recovering a biblical perspective."[75]

According to him, these writers owed much to the purging and enabling influence of the biblical revival. This was because most of their writings were shaped by the Bible's worldview.

73   *The Trumpet Sounds for Great Britain*, Vol 1, David E Gardner, p 85, Christian Foundation Publications, Cheshire UK, 1980
74   Ibid
75   *The Book That Made Your World*, Vishal Mangalwadi, p 270

They helped hold back the logical consequences of the Enlightenment's rejection of Revelation.

Examples of such poets include William Blake, William Wordsworth, Robert Browning, Lord Tennyson, Rudyard Kipling and John Masefield. Novelists consist of people like Sir Walter Scott, Charles Dickens, William Thackeray, the Bronte sisters and Robert Louis Stevenson.

Philanthropic and social service movements in England also owed their origins to the Great Awakening. As a result of the revival, men and women became consumed by the compassionate spirit of Jesus Christ. As their Lord and Saviour did, many of these men went out to rescue and bring relief to their fellow humans. Examples include Dr Barnardo's Homes, the Shaftesbury Society, the National Society for the Prevention of Cruelty to Children (NSPCC), the Salvation Army, the London City Mission, Muller's Homes, Fegan's Homes, The Pastoral Aid Society, National Children's Homes and Orphanages, the Boy Scouts, Girl Guides, Agnes Weston's Soldiers and Sailors Rest, YMCA, the forming of evening classes and Polytechnics, the Royal Society for Prevention of Cruelty to Animals (RSPCA) to mention these few.

It is a known fact that 99% of the people behind all these movements grew out of the evangelical revival which John Wesley and his associates led.

Another offshoot of the biblical revival was the emergence of the preaching tradition in the 19th century. Some of the great men that expounded the Bible during this age (rather than tell stories) include Charles Spurgeon, Nicholson Ryle, Danny James, etc. The Great Awakening further opened up the intelligent study of the Bible to the masses. It ultimately restored the Bible's position as the Book of Books of the Anglo-Saxon peoples.

Their biblical revival held in check the character-destroying consequences of atheism that corrupted other European nations like France.[76]

---

76   Ibid, p 271

Again, it should not be forgotten that the various missionary societies that inspired, raised and sent several hundred thousand young men and women to the uttermost parts of the earth were a product of the evangelical revival. Once the work of the revival had become established, several missionary societies were established, all within few years of each other.

I am sure that most people in the British Isles are unaware of the fact that British Trade Unionism was a direct product of the Great Awakening. The British Trade Unions actually grew out of the chapels.

Jack Lawson, a leading Trade Unionist who held office in the first Labour government of 1924, traced the origins of trade unionism origins to the chapels when he remarked,

> *"The evangelical revival of the eighteenth century*
> *saturated the industrial masses with a passion for*
> *a better life, personal, mental, moral and social.*
> *The chapel was their first social centre where they*
> *drew together, found strength in their weakness*
> *and expressed to each other their hidden thoughts*
> *and needs. Here men first found the language and*
> *art to express their antagonism to grim conditions*
> *and injustices.*
>
> *The most powerful force for the mental and moral*
> *elevation of the workers during the industrial era has*
> *been the chapels (contemptuously called 'Little Bethel'*
> *he said)."*[77]

The great Lloyd George also testified to the Christian origins of our Trade Unions when he said,

> *"John Wesley inaugurated a movement that gripped the*
> *soul of England, that deepened its spiritual instincts,*

77   *The Trumpet Sounds for Great Britain*, Vol 1, David E Gardner, p 90, Christian Foundation Publications, Cheshire UK, 1980

trained them and uplifted them. That movement which improved the conditions of the working classes in wages, in hours of labour and otherwise, found most of its best officers and non-commissioned officers in men trained in the Christian institutions which were the result of Wesley's Methodism.

I never realised the effect which Methodism has had upon the national character, so much as when I attended international congress, etc, and it is all due to the great religious revival of the 18th century."[78]

Time and space will fail me if I have to chronicle all the changes brought about in this great country and indeed the world at large as a result of the evangelical revival led by Wesley and his associates. On the far reaching effects of this revival, George Trevelyan, in his chronicles of the 19th century, declares,

"It was one of the turning points in the history of the world, then he said of Britain, after she had abolished the slave trade. Her command of the sea, her far flung empire, her mounting industrial power, her commercial supremacy, her inventive genius – above all, her increasing moral stature and her expanding spiritual vision won her a place of unique leadership amongst the nations, more than any other great nation in the middle of the 19th century. She was worthy of world power."[79]

Furthermore, it was because of this revival led by Wesley that the British people became known around the world as "The people of one Book", and that Book was the Bible.

Again it was also as a direct consequence of the influence from revivals that it was being said all over the world at that

---

78   Ibid
79   Ibid, page 97

time, "An Englishman's word is to be trusted, his word is his bond". This we pray will be repeated in our generation.

One-time American President, Calvin Coolidge, was not left out in making a remark about the impact that the revival had, not just on Britain, but also on America. He once remarked,

> *"America was born in a revival of religion, and at the back of it were John Wesley and George Whitefield."*[80]

No doubt even the sceptics, the agnostics, and the 21st century humanists will not argue that John Wesley left such an indelible mark on British history that can never be erased.

Making History

1. To live a life of influence requires commitment in little things. What is your daily routine like?

2. Talent is not enough. What character traits do you possess that can further enhance your gifts?

3. A revival starts with you. How much discipline do you exercise over your proclivities?

4. Can you identify and network with individuals, and organisations, which carry a vision and burden for societal transformation?

---

80   *Great Revivals*, Colin Whittaker, p 55, Marshall, Basingstoke, 1984

18 *WILLIAM TYNDALE*
The light bearer

"The entrance of your word gives light, it gives understanding to the simple."

(Psalm 119:130, NKJV)

"Be ashamed to die until you have won some victory for humanity."

Horace Mann (1796-1859),
American education reformist

"The Lord gave the word: great was the company of those that published it."

(Psalm 68:11, NKJV)

"It was not possible to establish the lay people in any truth except (that) the scriptures were so plainly laid before their eyes in their mother tongue."

William Tyndale

William Tyndale[81] (1494-1536) was an English scholar and translator who became a leading figure during the Protestant Reformation.

---

81 Taken from the book *A History of Britain*; Simon Schama, p 284, At The Edge of The World, 3000BC-1603 BBC, London, 2000

There were individuals who influenced him greatly through their written works. One of such persons was Desiderius Erasmus. An occurrence would take place, setting Tyndale on the path of history. It was around 1516, when Tyndale was still at Oxford. Erasmus' Greek New Testament Bible that was translated from Latin found its way from Holland to Oxford. At this time no such book had ever appeared before and those who could read Latin scrambled to buy themselves a copy.

Erasmus' burden and mission was for the Church to get back to the pure unadulterated Word of God. This conviction made a great impact on Tyndale.

The other personality who had a profound impact on Tyndale was Martin Luther, a German monk who himself was fed up with all the man-made traditions in the Church at the expense of the pure written Word of God.

Luther began to write for the necessity of change and his writings also began to arrive in England around 1517. It was under this milieu that William Tyndale studied. This was to have a profound impact on his life's mission.

So what kind of man was William Tyndale? He could be described as a visionary, a determined person who possessed the dogged ruggedness of a bulldog. He was very simple, single-minded, a great tactician and a strategic thinker. These are some of the qualities we need today for those would bring a radical change in our societies.

Professor Simon Schama has described him as,

> "...austere, unswerving, a little fanatical, but tireless in the pursuit of his mission... an astute tactician."[82]

---

82   Ibid

Background to Tyndale's Work

Present-day Christians might not fully appreciate the contributions of William Tyndale to our Christian faith in the nation (and the world at large), unless we know something about the state of our nation at that time.

As has been a major characteristic of our history over the centuries, Britain was spiritually in a dark state. We were spiritually bankrupt, darkness filled the land and gross darkness the people. The Church and state were under the bonds of Rome since the time of the Whitby Synod, with all its attendant evils. The traditions of men took precedence over the plain written Word of God.

To compound the problem, the masses were not only ignorant of the Word of God which could set them free, but they didn't have access to it in a language that they could comprehend.

Even amongst the priests of the day, large numbers were often ignorant of the Word while others didn't even trust the power therein. This period was aptly captured by the proverbial saying, "The blind leading the blind".

Professor David Daniel, one of the world's foremost authorities on William Tyndale, describes the pathetic condition in which many priests who were meant to be instructors and teachers of God's Word found themselves. He writes,

> "...some priests who knew little Latin would be glossing and allegorizing a few texts of scripture, twisting them into curious shapes that the church's centuries' old tradition of exegesis expected, and using Latin scriptures of course, which in places differed markedly (and conveniently) from the Greek originals."[83]

Vishal Mangalwadi writes further on the same issue:

83   *The Book That Made Your World*, Vishal Mangalwadi, p 150, Thomas Nelson, 2011

> *"Priests often twisted and disobeyed God's Word*
> *including the Ten Commandments. Many priests did not*
> *even know the Ten Commandments."*

In 1551, three decades after Tyndale's New Testament translation, a reforming Bishop Hooper made a shocking discovery in Gloucestershire, one of the godliest places in England.

> *"Of the unsatisfactory clergy, nine did not know how*
> *many commandments there were, 33 did not know where*
> *they appeared in the Bible (the gospel of Matthew was a*
> *favourable guess) and 168 could not repeat them."[84]*

Even the high nobility during this period were not spared from the Biblical illiteracy that pervaded our country. For example, the Duke of Norfolk is reputed to have remarked,

> *"I never read the scripture, nor ever will read it."[85]*

It was therefore in an atmosphere of spiritual darkness and stupor, coupled with political turmoil, that the contribution of William Tyndale can be appreciated.

Tyndale's Greatest Achievement

No doubt, William Tyndale's greatest achievement was making available the Word of God to the masses. Tyndale first voiced his life's mission when a priest advised him that,

> *"...we were better to be without God's Laws than*
> *the Popes."[86]*

---

84   Ibid, pp 150-151
85   *A History Of The English Speaking Peoples*, Vol 11, Winston Churchill, p 59, Cassell, London. 1956
86   *Foxe's Book of Martyrs*, Chapter XII

Tyndale's reply was,

> *"If God spare my life many years, I will cause a boy that
> driveth the plough shall know more of the scripture
> than thou dost."*[87]

To this mission he expended his time and resources, even to the point of risking his life.

At first, Tyndale approached Tunstall the Bishop of London, to help with the translation and printing of the Bible in English. This, in itself, was a rare privilege. Would the Bishop graciously take this offer and leave his name in the annals of history? Would he want to be seen as the one who sponsored and supported the printing of the Word of God for the masses in Tudor English, a language that they understood?

The Bishop turned Tyndale's offer down because the Church was very much uncomfortable with the idea of a Bible in Tudor English which would ultimately liberate the masses. Tyndale finally secured money from a rich merchant sympathizer who sent him abroad to get the job done.

In the late autumn of 1535 the Bible was printed in Tudor English. So great was the demand for the new translation of the Bible that within a short span Tyndale's translation and Coverdale's were running into several editions.

However, this initiative he took in translating the Bible (that the masses could comprehend and be set free from superstition and traditions of men) cost him his life.

In October 1536 he was burnt at the stake. Like the first Christian martyr, Stephen, he prayed a simple prayer as the flames burnt. His last words were,

> *"Lord, open the King of England's eyes!"*

---

87   *The Acts and Monuments of John Foxe*, Vol. 5, John Foxe, p 117, London R. B.
     Seeley and W..Burnside, 1837-1841

Indeed it didn't take long for God to answer the prayers of His servant. Barely a year after this incident, a copy of the Bible was to be chained to the lectern of every church in Britain. The instigation was at the order of none other than His Royal Highness King Henry VIII himself.

The parishioners now had access to the Bible, in a language they could comprehend. Six copies were sent to St Paul's in the city of London. It was said, especially, that any person with an audible voice for the purpose of reading it aloud was sought after.[88]

As I read through the pages of history about the enormous price that our forebears and heroes of faith paid to give us the Bible today, I am not only eternally grateful, but also convicted. For it seems to me that present-day Christians take the ownership of a Bible for granted.

How I wish all Christians were reminded regularly, and indeed our nation, of the price such people like William Tyndale paid.

William Tyndale, Britain and indeed the whole English-speaking world should be eternally grateful for the price of giving us the Word of God.

Another fact is also worth mentioning for the purpose of highlighting the significance of Tyndale's effort. Almost 500 years after his work, much of his translation is still with us today. Despite the high quality of translators who converged to create the King James Version in 1611, they eventually ended up using about 90% of Tyndale's version of the New Testament. Of the Old Testament version, around 90% of his work was also used.

Furthermore, as a result of Tyndale's translation of the Bible, the King now ordered everywhere in the country to teach their parishioners how to read the Bible.

---

88   *A History of The English Speaking Peoples,* Winston Churchill, Vol. II, p 61

Making History

1. A habit of study develops a sense of purpose. Do you invest in books or are you apathetic about study?

2. A deep conviction of purpose is a driving force in the face of intense adversity. What problem do you believe you have a solution to in your neighbourhood?

3. Who are you influenced by in your life? Do such influences add to your wellbeing or subtract from you?

4. Can you list three history makers that inspire you? Remember that if no-one inspires you, you will soon expire!

19 *SELINA HASTINGS The matriach of Methodism*

"Only a life lived for others is a life worthwhile."
Albert Einstein (1879-1955),
German-born

"Whoever wants to be great must become a servant."
(Mark 10:43)

The Message

Without doubt, the 18th century revival that swept all across the British Isles is arguably the most important phenomenon in our history. This is not only because of the national transformation that it brought in its wake; its impact and residue still resonate very much in our society today.

Whenever we study Church history and observe those used by God as vessels, we normally expect to come across courageous men, particularly those with extraordinary leadership skills. Furthermore, when we read about the 18th century Great Awakening, two men stand out as catalysts. These men were George Whitefield and John Wesley.

However, it must be said that while this may be true, the two men were by no means the only ones used by God. There were several others that many of us either might have ignored or are yet to discover.

One of such persons was an outstanding figure born into nobility, Selina, Countess of Huntingdon. She was born on the 24th of August 1707 and died on the 17th of June 1791.

Her family lived in Northamptonshire in the British Midlands. She didn't have a happy childhood as her parents separated when she was only six. At the age of twenty one, Selina married Theophilus Hastings, the Earl of Huntingdon, in 1728. Through this union, she became a Countess.

She was such a central figure in the 18th century that Horace Walpole called her the matriarch of the Methodists.

Furthermore, John Henry Newman (the Roman Catholic) comments on her outstanding life,

> "She devoted herself, her means, her time, her thoughts, to the cause of Christ. She did not spend her money on herself. She did not allow the homage paid to her rank to remain with herself. She was clearly a pivotal figure in the evangelical revival."[89]

Her Conversion

A similarity has been drawn between Selina, the Countess of Huntington, and Lydia, the seller of purple in the Book of Acts *"whose heart the Lord opened"* (Acts 16:14). Both women were clearly gifted and very religious. However, neither of them knew nor experienced the saving grace of Jesus, until the light quietly dawned upon them.

Two major factors facilitated her conversion. First was her sister-in-law, Lady Margaret Hastings. Like Martin Luther before, who found faith in Christ, the Countess of

89   Wikipedia

Huntington put in so much effort in order to "work out her own salvation". The more she engaged in this endeavour, the more peace and assurance of faith eluded her. This was contrary to the experience of her sister-in-law, who possessed peace and joy.

Secondly, like many others over the century, a serious crisis occurred when she became very sick and even her life was threatened.

This serious illness made her despondent. Therefore, when she and her sister-in-law heard the Gospel faithfully preached in Yorkshire by a certain Mr Ingham, she was deeply touched and then publicly confessed her faith in Christ alone. This happened around 1738.

It is worth noting that the change which followed her confession of faith in Christ was very dramatic. She took every conceivable opportunity to testify about her new-found faith, particularly to the nobility. She also did everything possible to encourage the spread of the gospel as fast and far as possible.

So what was her specific contribution and legacy towards the British nation?

The Good News To The Nobility

".... which was with the deputy of the country, Sergius Paulus, a prudent man, who called for Barnabas and Saul, and desired to hear the word of God."

(Acts 13:7, KJV)

"There was a man of the Pharisees, named Nicodemus, a ruler of the Jews: The same came to Jesus by night..."

(John 3:1-2a, KJV)

"And He said unto them, "Go ye into all the world, and preach the gospel to every creature."

(Mark 16:15, KJV)

That the gospel is meant for every creature is not something that the Bible leaves us in doubt about. Jesus' last command to his disciples was to preach the Good News to every creature, irrespective of their economic or social standing in the community.

Over the centuries, it might appear as if the rich, famous and those of the nobility have largely been neglected when it comes to preaching the Gospel to them.

Some have argued from the records of Luke that the Good News was actually not just for the poor in spirit, but those who were financially destitute.

I believe to take this stand is to ignore the example set by Jesus and Paul, who both ministered to the rich and famous, and even testified in the greatest courts of their day.

Selina, Countess of Huntingdon, was to follow in the footsteps of her Saviour. If there was one lesson and legacy she left behind (which I strongly believe the 21st century Church must emulate), it was this: she knew the strategic importance of reaching out to the movers and shakers of society.

No doubt there were preceding organisations like the Full Gospel Business Men's Fellowship. Their primary objective was to target professionals and highly placed individuals in society with the Gospel of Jesus Christ. The atmosphere would be in a very relaxed and non-threatening environment, often over a meal with a very "popular" speaker preaching the message.

The Countess, on her part, used her position to influence many of the nobility to hear the Gospel. She was particularly anxious that they listen to George Whitefield's sermons. Ann Frankland, the daughter of the Earl of Scarborough, was one of the first among the aristocracy to be converted as a result of listening to Whitefield's sermons.

Selina maintained close relationship with many of the ladies in the court. She would accompany them to gospel meetings.

Alfred New aptly captures the Countess's influence on the nobility of her day when he writes,

> *"The good effected by the efforts of Lady Huntingdon was very great, and through her persuasions, members of the aristocracy were brought within the sound of the preaching of the Gospel. She embraced every opportunity of speaking on religious subjects to her friends in her mansions and her manners were so polished, her much sought after, notwithstanding her religion.*
>
> *Her drawing rooms in town were crowded with doctors, poets, philosophers, statesmen, lords, and ladies, where the great truths of religion were discussed and her ladyship not infrequently astonished those present by the clearness and force of her views of Truth."*[90]

This is a great lesson and inspiration to many who are from the nobility professing Christianity today, or those who have the privilege of accessing and relating with the *crème de la crème* of society.

It must be pointed out that Selina's influence was not only restricted to the nobility and wealthy, as might be misconstrued. Nothing could be farther from the truth. Though she dined and wined with Kings and Queens, she never lost her common touch. It has been said of her that "Her drawing rooms were fitted with brilliant assemblies, her kitchen was crowded with the poor, to whom she dispensed her charities for the relief of their wants, and directed them to Jesus Christ as the only remedy for their guilt".

90   *The Elect Lady*, Gilbert W. Kirby, published by the Trustees of the Countess of Huntingdon's Connexion, 1972

Quite regularly George Whitefield preached twice a week in the drawing room of the Countess's town house, thereby demonstrating a strategic use of her home and influence for the advancement of the Gospel.

In one of Whitefield's letters he wrote,

> *"Good Lady Huntingdon is come to town: and I am to preach at her Ladyship's house twice a week to the great and noble. O that some of them may be effectually called and taste of the riches of redeeming love."*[91]

Whitefield was not the only popular preacher of his day who preached for Selina. Others included Wesley, Venn, Romaise, Fletcher, Toplady, to mention a few.

It should be mentioned that Selina's influence was not only linked to the English nobility. She was also well acquainted with some of Scottish nobility who had been converted through Whitefield's preaching and when they came to London, they invariably visited her. It is worthy of note to mention that the Countess was instrumental in starting a meeting for prayer and Bible study for ladies of noble birth. Some of the people who attended these meetings were among the outstanding names of the time.

Inspired by her example, many other titled ladies opened their drawing-rooms for evangelistic meetings. One of such persons converted through the efforts of the Countess was Lady Glenorchy, who was destined to become the "Selina" of Scotland.

91   Ibid

The Countess and Her Chapels

The sequence of events leading to the establishment of chapels established by the Countess could be regarded as incidental rather than the product of design or intent.

It was a well known fact that the Countess was a committed member of the established Church and it was never her intention to secede from it. However, many of the "Methodists" whom the Countess befriended had already been expelled from their churches because of their evangelistic zeal and were driven to preach in the open air or in the streets.

It was under these circumstances that the Countess felt the need to begin the establishment of chapels in different locations. They would serve as preaching stations for such men and where new converts might be built up in the faith.

The first of such chapels was built in Brighton. She was said to have sold her jewels to the tune of about £698 to acquire this chapel in 1761.

In all, it is said the Countess established sixty four churches with her personal finances and contributed funds to many more, a testament to her sacrificial lifestyle and disposition.

It is worth noting that this feat was something unknown in the 18th century. At that time it was unheard of for a woman to lead a Christian denomination. Even in present times, women with such a record are few and far between. The reason could be that Christianity is still grappling with the issue of women in leadership and ordination.

I wonder how many women we know today who lead a denomination with at least 64 churches under them.

This is very much unknown in several parts of Africa experiencing massive church growth!

It is reported that the Countess expended at least £100,000 on religious works. This amount would be worth several million pounds today.

Any lessons and legacy for the 21st century Church? I believe a lot.

Here is a great example we can follow. Woman, you can become all that God destined you to be. You can be used by God to expand and extend the Kingdom of God. To ministers of God, particularly the men, it is time we released the women (particularly those strategically positioned by God) to reach their own kind.

The Countess and Her College

> *"Then He said to his disciples, 'The harvest truly is plentiful, but the laborers are few. Therefore pray the lord of the harvest to send out labourers into His harvest.'"*
>
> (Matthew 9:37-38, NKJV)

Perhaps one of the greatest achievements and legacy that the Countess of Huntingdon left was the establishment of a College for training ministers of the Gospel.

As a person with a strong passion for the conversion of people to Christ, her enthusiasm knew no bounds. She personally received invitations from all across the country for soul winning, but as Jesus remarked, the labourers were few. For this reason, recruited labourers needed to be trained.

The interest of the Countess in training men for the ministry stemmed from her support of a college in America, which had been founded for this purpose. Furthermore, England, Oxford and Cambridge were still the only places where men could train for the ministry and these universities were closed to dissenters.

In response to this challenge, the inspiration from America and the need to advance the cause of the Gospel made her seek the Lord's face in prayer. After much prayer, she came to the conclusion that the answer was to establish a College where men could be trained for the ministry.

The Bible College was established at Trevecca, in Mid Wales. Later, in 1792, the College moved to Hertfordshire and was renamed Cheshunt College. In 1906, it was moved to Cambridge and merged with Westminster College, a part of Cambridge University.

Like Charles Spurgeon, Lady Huntingdon gave liberally of her time and energies to maintain the work of the College throughout her lifetime. It is worthy of note that students from this College did much evangelizing and church planting throughout England.

Other legacies of Selina, Countess of Huntingdon, were through the formation of her connections. In the 18th century there was a tradition of bringing together evangelical leaders closely connected or associated with a religious cause. Thus, the Countess built up over the year a connection comprising such men. These ministers of the Gospel occupied her pulpits and other ministers rallied round her.

Those associated with this connection included eminent men such as George Whitefield, Sacrithy Fletcher, Vicar of Madeley and first President of the Countess's College, Augustus Toplady (Fletcher's antagonist in doctrinal controversy and author of the popular Hymn "Rock of Ages").

Others include Henry Venn, first curate of Clapham in London, sacristy John-Berridge Grimshaw, James Hervey, William Romaine, Thomas Hawes, the Hon. Walter Sherley and many others. This was no doubt a remarkable collection of powerful men and women who exercised great influence in their day. Gilbert W. Kirby has remarked that,

> *"There can hardly have been since apostolic days a connection comparable with that associated with the countess."*[92]

---

92   Ibid

Furthermore, the Countess was very much interested in missionary work. When the slaves who fought for the British were granted their freedom after the American War of Independence, students who had been at Trevecca went to minister to them in Nova Scotia. Some of these freed slaves returned to Africa in 1792, to Freetown Sierra Leone. On arrival they started churches of their original denominations.

This was how the Countess of Huntingdon's connection in Sierra Leone began. It was not until 1839 that the line of communication was established between the two connections. It is noteworthy that a strong bond has existed between them both ever since.

At her death in 1791, there were well over sixty causes associating themselves with her, even though most of these were in local trusts.

Making History

1. A privileged life is also an opportunity to spread the Gospel in your social class. What methods do you employ to minister the Gospel to the rich and powerful?

2. Wealth is through God's grace. How do you manifest this grace in your conduct as a wealthy person?

3. Does your status as a person of wealth spur you to spread the Gospel or are you concerned about the responses of those in your circle of influence?

4. Can you identify a project that you can give your wealth and energies to that will be your lasting legacy?

THE FAMILY AND
RELIGIOUS SPHERE

Chapter 20
Mary Mitchell Slessor *Missionary and social reformer*

Chapter 21
Dr. Thomas Barnardo *The social enterpreneur*

20 MARY MITCHELL SLESSOR
Missionary and social reformer

||||||||||||||||||||||||| |||||||||||||||||||||||||||||||||||||||||||||||||||||||||||||||||||||||||||||||||||||||||||||

"The smallest things are as absolutely necessary as the great things. It were worthwhile to die, if thereby a soul could be born again."

Mary Mitchell Slessor (1848-1915),
Scottish missionary to Nigeria

"Let your roots go down into Christ and draw up nourishment from him. See that you go on growing in the Lord and become strong and vigorous in the truth."

(Colossians 2:7, The Living Bible)

Mary Mitchell Slessor was born on the 2nd of December 1848 in Aberdeen.

Her father, Robert, was a cobbler. Her mother was an only child, brought up in a home of refinement and piety. She is described by those who knew her as a sweet-faced woman, patient, gentle and retiring with a deeply religious disposition.

On Timothy's spiritual legacy, Paul, the Apostle from Tarsus, declared,

"When I call to remembrance the genuine faith that is in you which dwelt first in your grandmother Lois and your mother Eunice, and I am persuaded is in you also."

(2 Timothy 1:5, NKJV)

Mary Slessor seems to have enjoyed a similar heritage, particularly from her mother. This would shape her destiny in the coming years. Even Mary Slessor herself claimed that much of her godly character and her upbringing were as a result of her mother's godly influence. She once remembered,

"I owe a great debt of gratitude to my sainted mother."[93]

On the other hand, her father was an alcoholic. This lifestyle brought a great deal of misery, poverty and strife into their family.

Mary Slessor's working career started very early at the age of 10. Not long afterwards, she became the primary breadwinner of the house. She was a person whose life was characterised by sacrifice and self-denial. This virtue would define her adult life as a Missions Stateswoman.

Mary Slessor became a Christian at a very tender age. She deeply loved going to church. Church provided her a place to escape from the miserable home life she experienced. She also loved reading the Bible, particularly the Gospels, soaking up everything she could read about her Saviour Jesus Christ!

In my study of history makers, be it from the Holy Book or secular history, one indispensable characteristic that they all possessed was vision. They were all great dreamers.

"Where there is no vision the people perish."

(Proverbs 29:18, KJV)

"Where there is no revelation the people cast off restraint."

(Proverbs 29:18, NKJV)

"Behold this dreamer cometh." [Joseph's brothers on Joseph]

(Genesis 37:19, KJV)

"It was the dream of my girlhood to be a pioneer missionary."

Mary Slessor

Mary Slessor, from her childhood, had always dreamt and desired to be used by God in a foreign field. The opportunity presented itself when John, her brother, died. Their mother had hoped he would become a missionary. It was as if she was next in line for missionary work. Again the death of David Livingstone inspired scores of people in Britain to desire a missionary vocation. Mary Slessor was one of such persons.

In 1875, Slessor applied and was accepted by the Calabar Mission to Nigeria. At the age of twenty seven and in the summer of 1876, she sailed for Calabar. It was a place long known for its slave trade and deadly environment. A few comments need to be made at this stage.

First, it is important to commend the bold step the Calabar Mission took in recruiting a single young woman for foreign mission. This was very uncommon in those days. Exploration and pioneer work were no ready options for a single female missionary until Mary Slessor arrived on the scene. This is also a lesson to modern day ministers and ministries. They deny women, perhaps the most versatile force in God's Kingdom, the opportunity of serving the Kingdom and thereby fulfilling their God ordained destinies.

Secondly, without a shadow of doubt, no one would have read the history of Marry Slessor's exploits in Africa without coming to the unreserved conclusion that she was involved in apostolic work.

On arrival in Calabar, Duke Town was Marry Slessor's first port of call. Here she spent her time teaching in a Mission School and ministering in nearby villages. However, in her own words, life here was too much of a routine and very much predictable. She was not someone given to all the social niceties and the comfortable lifestyle of the missionary families she encountered while in Duke Town.

"And so I have made it my aim to preach the gospel, not where Christ was named, lest I should build on another man's foundation."

(Romans 15:20, NKJV)

"To preach the gospel in the regions beyond you, and not to boast in another man's sphere of accomplishment."

(2 Corinthians 10:16, NKJV)

Mary Slessor was a pioneer, a trail blazer. She ventured to places that even men were afraid to go. Her fearlessness and doggedness would earn her the name, *The White Queen of Calabar*. Her heart was always set on doing pioneer work in the interior. She, however, had to return to Britain for treatment of malaria. For three years she had several bouts of malaria and other tropical diseases. During her convalescence in Britain, she earnestly yearned to be reunited with her family and friends. She eventually returned to Africa, refreshed and excited about her new assignment at the old town, three miles further inland along the Calabar River.

Here she was free to maintain her own lifestyle, living in a mud hut and eating local produce. She was also now involved in a variety of tasks which included mediating in disputes, dispensing medication, supervising schools, and mothering unwanted children. Like John Wesley and other great preachers, Mary Slessor became a circuit preacher. On Sundays, she would travel several miles through the jungle, from village to village, sharing the gospel with those who would listen.

She would be back again in Africa in 1885. By now, she was more determined to penetrate even further into the interior villages. No sooner had she resumed her missionary work that she received news of her beloved mother's death. In less than three months, her sister also died. She was left all alone because, during her furlough, one of her sisters had also died. Now there were no more close ties in Britain. Often, she would be overwhelmed by despondency and loneliness. Indeed, she paid a heavy price for serving her Master and His Kingdom.

Once she wrote,

> *"There is no one to write and tell all my stories and troubles and nonsense to."*

In August 1888, Slessor went down towards Okoyoung. This was a remote area that had claimed the lives of other missionaries who dared penetrate its borders. She, however, went with the assistance of her friend, King Eyo of Old Town.

Mary Slessor was a pioneer missionary, educationist, social reformer, a fearless judge, and a mother to unwanted babies.

For anyone to appreciate the legacy and contributions she made, it is crucial that we first have an idea of the prevailing circumstances in Calabar. These circumstances will indicate the state of affairs before she got there and the changes and reform that her presence and ministry brought about.

Calabar is located on the southern coast of Nigeria. Calabar was totally given to witchcraft and spiritism, violence, ritual killings and tribal wars abounded everywhere. Cruel tribal customs were deeply embedded in tradition, which were responsible for claiming several precious souls.

Injustice, particularly to the socially disadvantaged, was predominant. This was the social milieu that Mary Slessor met in Calabar!

In his monumental work, *Mary Slessor, The White Queen of Calabar*, Eugene Myers Harrison recalls an interesting story. He recounts how a tree fell on Etim, an heir apparent of a certain Chief Edem.

This seeming accident would however threaten to spark off violence as a result of silly superstition. Harrison narrates how Mary Slessor's intervention was able to rescue several souls and prevent a bloodbath!

"Run, Ma! Run!" Whenever 'Ma', the white woman, heard these words she knew that serious trouble was brewing so she hurried out of the house and down the path into the forest. Presently, she found Etim, the oldest son and heir apparent of Chief Edem, lying unconscious under a tree which had fallen on him. For a fortnight she nursed him in his mother's house, but her efforts were in vain.

Early one Sunday morning, while she was resting in her own hut, the boy's life began to ebb away. This news sent a spasm of terror throughout the district, for every violent death was attributed to witchcraft and it was certain that a number of persons would be put to death on the charge of having caused the tree to fall on the boy. Hurrying to the Chief's house, Mary Slessor found the natives blowing smoke into the dying lad's nostril, shouting into his ears and rubbing ground pepper into his eyes. As soon as life had fled, the chief shouted: "Sorcerers have killed my son and they must die! Bring the witch-doctor!"

At these words, everybody fled when the witchdoctor arrived. He tried out his divinations and placed the responsibility for the boy's death on a certain village. Thereafter, armed warriors marched to the village in particular, seized a dozen men and women, brought them

*back loaded with chains and fastened them to posts in
the yard.*

*The Chief endeavoured to persuade Ma to let the
prisoners submit to the 'poison ordeal' for, said he, "If they
are not guilty, they will not die". Mary Slessor knew that the
poison would kill them, irrespective of their innocence, and
refused to agree.*

*Finally, eleven of the prisoners were released and the
death of the one remaining, a woman, was demanded.
When Mary Slessor stubbornly refused, the Chief stormed,
threatened to burn down the house, and in blazing passion
declared, "She caused my son's death and she must die!"
Bowing her head, Mary Slessor prayed for strength and
patience and love. And, after several days of terrific strain,
she eventually won. The last of the prisoners was released
and the Chief contented himself with the sacrifice of a cow.
It was the first time in this entire district that a Chief's grave
had not been saturated with human blood."*[94]

This story may sound like one typical of a movie but this was
the practice in Calabar when Mary Slessor arrived. Did she bring
about change? Did she impose Kingdom culture on a generation
in which life was characterised by wicked superstition?

One question kept recurring in my heart; where are the
modern day heroines like Slessor? Who will reform our
ailing society and take their place in the annals of Church
history? Who says a woman cannot be a powerful tool for
societal transformation?

Again, what many of us and indeed most people will count as
a blessing from God, the birth of twins, was believed to be a curse,
until Mary Slessor arrived in Calabar. In many cases, one or both
twins were killed, and the mother exiled to an area reserved
for outcasts. Slessor not only rescued twins numbering up to

94   *Mary Slessor, The White Queen of Calabar*, Eugene Myers, Harrison, www.
wholesomewords.org

several hundred, but she also fought the perpetrators. In some instances her life was at risk. Let us consider yet another story to appreciate what she actually did and how the White Queen of Calabar brought an end to the ungodly killing of twins.

> "One day there was a great sadness in Mary's village.
> 'What's wrong?', she asked the women. 'My sister has had twins...', a sad-faced African woman said, '...so the babies will be killed and she'll be chased 'away into the bush.'
> 'What!!!', roared Mary, jumping to her feet. 'Take me to her!' The poor woman hesitated. 'Now!'
>
> There was a huddle of people around the hut. As long as she was there, Mary knew the babies were safe.
>
> 'Explain what's happening', she pleaded.
>
> 'When twin babies are born one of them is the child of an evil spirit. But, as we don't know which one, they are both killed. And because the mother has had a spirit child, she's put out in the bush to be killed by wild animals' replied one of the women.
>
> 'No, she is not!' There was no arguing with Mary Slessor. 'I will look after the twins!' she said.
>
> 'Just wait and see what happens. Neither of them is the child of an evil spirit. The Lord God made them both!'"

Because of Mary's anger and determination, the woman survived and so did the children. Mary was gathering quite a little family around her. The villagers were impressed that there didn't seem to be evil spirits in the babies. News about her heroic stand spread and eventually the people of Calabar stopped the practice of leaving mothers delivered of twins to die out in the bush and also stopped killing twins.[95]

This story depicts what I call societal transformation through the Gospel of the Kingdom!

---

95 *Ten Girls Who Changed the World*, Irene Howat, pp 75-76, Christian Focus Publications, Ross-Shire, Scotland, Britain, 2011

What Mary Slessor did is what Jesus expects of His true followers. To be the salt and the light of their societies! (Matt 5:14-16). Today most Christians are content with just being the light of the Church.

It is not meant to be that way. Our vocation is outside the four walls of the Church. It seems to me that rather than go outside and impact society like Mary Slessor did, a lot of Christians are being held hostage in the Church by their pastors and elders!

Mary Slessor's pioneering activities were not just limited to preaching the gospel. Her actions extended to social advocacy; she stopped the killing of twins and their mothers. This changed many wicked age-old traditions.

She also earned the reputation of being a peacemaker. This got her an appointment as a judge in the Okoyong area of Calabar. In 1891, she was also appointed the first Vice-Consul to Okoyong, a government position she held for many years. In that capacity, she acted as a judge and presided over court cases involving land disputes, debt cases, and family matters. Her methods were unconventional by British standards. She would often refuse to act solely on the evidence before her if she was personally aware of other factors. Nevertheless, her methods were well suited to African society.[96]

Mary Slessor was isolated from outsiders for much of her mission career. However, in 1893 she enjoyed a visit from Mary Kingsley, a British journalist, who would later on write *Travels in West Africa*. Even though Kingsley confessed that she was not a Christian, she greatly admired her hostess and the impact her life had made in Calabar. The writings of this self-confessed unbeliever seem to give us a glimpse into the life and legacy of the White Queen of Calabar.

---

96   *From Jerusalem to Irian Jaya*, Ruth A Tucker, p 173, Zondervan, Michigan, USA
     2004

She writes,

> *"This very wonderful lady has been eighteen years in Calabar, for the last six or seven living entirely alone, as far as white folks go, in a clearing, in the forest near one of the principal villages of the Okoyong district, and ruling as a veritable white chief over the entire district. Her great abilities, both physical and intellectual, have given her among the savage tribe a unique position, and won her, from white and black who know her, a profound esteem. Her knowledge of the native, his language, his way of thought, his disease, his difficulties, and all that is his, is extraordinary, and the amount of good she has done, no man can fully estimate. Okoyong, when she went there alone....... was given, as most of the surrounding districts still are, to killing at funerals, ordeal by poison, and perpetual internecine wars. Many of these evil customs she has stamped out.. Mrs Slessor stands alone."*[97]

After about 40 years of labour in Africa, Mary Slessor died in her hut on the 13th of January 1915, at the age of 66. Nevertheless, she left a permanent legacy in the annals of history.

Dr Robert H. Glover, missionary statesman, teacher, and author, in his book, *The Progress Of World-Wide Missions*, describes the life and work of Mary Slessor in the following brief words.

> *"Her life rivals, in many particulars, that of David Livingstone. She served in Africa under the United Free Church of Scotland from 1876 to 1915. From an unlettered factory girl in the homeland, she advanced*

---

97   Ibid

into the foremost rank of missionary pathfinders. Her work was that of a pioneer among the most savage tribes of the Calabar Hinterland. She singlehandedly tamed and transformed three pagan communities in succession. It is a question if the career of any other woman missionary has been marked by so many strange adventures, daring feats, signal providences and wonderful achievements."[98]

Perhaps, it might be best to conclude this study on Mary Slessor's achievements and legacy by quoting J. H. Morrison, when he paid tribute to her,

"She is entitled to a place in the front ranks of the heroines of history, and if goodness be counted an essential element of true greatness, if eminence be reckoned by love and self-sacrifice, by years of endurance and suffering by a life of sustained heroism and purest.'

Making History

1. Taking a stand requires taking risks. Are you prepared for such demands?

2. Sacrifice is very demanding in its true sense. Are you willing to make it happen?

3. When all hell seems to break loose, do you give up or do push on?

4. Can you identify one important trait or virtue that makes Marry Slessor stand out as a historical personality?

---

98   *Mary Slessor, Among the Cannibals of Calabar,* Thomas John Bach, www. wholesomewords.org

CHAPTER

21 Dr. THOMAS BARNARDO
The social enterpreneur

> "We have a responsibility in our time, as others have
> had in theirs, not to be prisoners of history but to shape
> history, a responsibility to fill the role of path-finder,
> and to build with others a global network of purpose
> and law."
>
> Madeleine Albright (born May 15, 1937),
> First woman to become the United States Secretary of State

> "The main business is not to see what lies dimly at a
> distance but to do what lies clearly at hand."
>
> Thomas Carlyle (1795-1881),
> Scottish philosopher, essayist, and historian

Thomas Barnardo was the fourth child of six children born to
John and Abigail Barnardo. He was born and raised in one of
the poorest district of Dublin. His father (John) was a furrier
who ran a shop and supplied the carriage industry. Some
writers indicate that his childhood was stormy and far from
being happy. His schooling included Sunday School, Parish Day
School and St. Patricks Cathedral Grammar School, Dublin.

A very significant milestone in Thomas Barnardo's life was
his conversion to the Christian faith on the 26th of May 1862,

175

at the age of sixteen. Soon after his conversion, he became very active in church life, teaching Bible classes and home-visiting.

Like many history makers before him, his commitment to social work was strengthened when he heard Hudson Taylor speaking in Dublin about the work of the China Inland Mission. Barnardo's Christian beliefs also inspired him in deciding to become a medical missionary in China.

In order to actualize this dream, he set out for London to train as a medical doctor.

Travels, sometimes, have a way of enabling one to accomplish destiny. This was true of Jesus during His ministry on earth as He travelled from one place to another.

> *"Then Jesus went about all the cities and villages, teaching in their synagogues, preaching the gospel of the Kingdom, and healing every sickness and every disease among the people. But when He saw the multitudes, He was moved with compassion for them, because they were weary and scattered, like sheep having no shepherd. Then He said to His disciples, "The harvest truly is plentiful, but the labourers are few."*
>
> (Matthew 9:37, NKJV)

Thomas Barnardo had a similar experience like Jesus. On getting to London to pursue his study in medicine, what he saw and experienced made a lasting impact on his soul.

So, what was the London that Barnardo arrived in like? The year was 1866, a city struggling to cope with the effects of the Industrial Revolution. The population had doubled between 1821 and 1851 and doubled yet again before the end of the century. Much of this increase was concentrated in the East End; overcrowding, bad housing, unemployment, poverty and disease were rife in these parts. One in five children died before their fifth birthday.

Furthermore, a few months after Barnardo came to London, an outbreak of cholera swept through the East End, killing more than 3,000 people and leaving many families destitute.

According to the 'Poor Law' operating during those times, the only recourse for the suffering families was to go to the Workhouse. This, however, was too humiliating for many. Rather than go to the workhouse, they tried to survive on the streets. This resulted in several thousand children sleeping on the streets. To make matters worse, many more were forced to beg after being maimed in the factories.

This was the dark social challenge that confronted Thomas Barnado as he arrived in London. What did he do? How did he respond? First, he began to visit homes of the poor and to comfort the dying. His attention, inevitably, was drawn to their plight and needs.

He began to preach in beer houses and on street corners. This often met with serious attacks, including being pelted with rotten eggs. On one occasion, he even suffered two broken ribs.

As I read the pages of history, I am greatly challenged by what many of our modern-day heroes of faith have suffered for the sake of the Kingdom.

I am too ashamed to compare scenarios similar to that of Thomas Barnardo, the challenges, obstacles, and persecutions, with the scenarios we are confronted with today. Yet many of us are complaining and fainting in our hearts.

A life-changing experience would eventually have a profound effect on his passion for ministry. A young local lad from around the East End of London, Jim Jarvis, had made a striking impression on him. Barnardo saw firsthand the appalling conditions many children lived under; they slept on rooftops and in sewers.

This experience spurred his decision to drop his ambition of travelling to China and devote himself, instead, to helping destitute children.

As you are reading this account, carefully consider my challenge to you. What is the social problem in your community, city, or nation, which God is providentially drawing your attention to? How will you respond?

Remember that it does not matter how much real estate and landed property you acquire, academic degrees you have earned, and how much money you have in the bank. What society will remember you for is how many lives you impacted and changed.

Ask yourself this question: 'What solution have I been called to bring to the problems of my community or nation?'

Again, at a time a high percentage of Christians believe they have to travel several thousand miles in order to do mission, one fact is overlooked. There are missionary opportunities on our doorsteps. Jesus Christ even affirmed,

"For the poor you have with you always."
(John 12:8a, NKJV)

One of the first steps that Dr Barnardo took after his visit was to establish a Ragged School. The first opened in 1870 on Stepney Causeway. It was for boys only.

Today, most church leaders, deacons, elders and the majority of Christians will stay in their stained glass church buildings, shutting their eyes to the plight of the socially ostracized in our society. Back then, Thomas Barnardo would regularly go out at night, into the slum district, to find destitute children.

The story is told that one evening an 11 year old boy, John Somers, nicknamed 'Carrots', was turned away because the shelter was totally full. Two days later, he was found dead from malnutrition and exposure. From then on, his homes bore the sign:

"No Destitute Child Ever Refused Admission"

At a time when several organisations imposed restrictions on the kind of children they admitted, Barnardo Homes were very radical in their approach. They were a fore-runner in equal opportunities for children, no matter their background and circumstances. Barnardo refused to discriminate between the 'deserving' and 'undeserving' poor. He accepted all children including black, disabled and 'illegitimate'.

It must be mentioned that through this Christian charity Barnardo pioneered a number of schemes in our nation. One was the scheme for children with disabilities. How did they achieve this? First they searched for foster and adoptive homes for children with severe disabilities. Later on, they ran projects that successfully brought profoundly disabled children out of long stay hospitals to live in small, community based units. Alongside, they also started schemes to support families caring for disabled children at home.

Barnardo and Children's Education

One of the enduring legacies of Dr Barnardo was his establishment of Ragged Schools. The schools were both located in Hope Place, one for boys and the other for girls. A highly educated man himself, he profoundly understood the importance of educating a child. This education was geared towards lifting destitute children from poverty. Within a few years of commencing the school, they became very successful; the numbers attending began to grow in leaps and bounds.

Thomas Barnardo was a great strategist and fund raiser. He used his network of relationships to raise money for his cause. A number of his donors and partners included bankers. As the numbers increased, he soon raised money and rented some canal-side warehouses located at 46 Copperfield Road, Stepney. These warehouses were converted into a school.

The Copperfield Road Ragged School opened in 1876. It was aimed at children aged five to ten years. It is worth noting that this school soon became the largest Ragged Day School in London. By 1896, the records showed there were some 1,075 children attending the day school.[99]

Unlike the kind of education that many children receive today, Barnardo only offered elementary education, but they were expected to take some form of job training.

A Hebrew proverb says that if you don't teach your child a trade, you teach them to steal. It is therefore not surprising that despite being a preacher and teacher, Paul was a tent-maker. Following Biblical precedent, boys were trained for manual jobs like electricians, and gardening, while the girls were encouraged to learn domestic duties. This is a legacy that I believe is worth emulating in the 21st century.

Barnardo Homes

As mentioned earlier, Thomas Barnardo is famously remembered more for the provision of homes for destitute children. The first opened on Stepney Causeway in 1870.

One of the outstanding characteristics of these homes was that they taught enterprise. In a day when one of the greatest burdens of modern governments in Britain is tackling unemployment, we need to borrow a leaf from Barnardo on how he approached this problem. Today, there are tens of thousands who prefer to depend on government handouts than to work. Barnardo homes taught the children self–reliance, responsibility and discipline. He set up different small-scale businesses which paid them wages. The businesses had departments including small wood-chopping, brush making, boot making and tract-making departments. They all employed these children.

The children were raised in a disciplined environment. They were expected to rise early, and spend hours doing chores,

99   http://www.infed.org.thinkers/banado.htm

cleaning and tidying their rooms, digging and planting in the garden and carrying out maintenance work.

On the activities of the home, particularly its entrepreneurial spirit, Rose writes,

> *"He built workshops, fitted workrooms, started a city messenger's brigade, brush making and boot making departments and a tract department for the sale of improving literature. He opened up a new Branch Ragged School in Salmon Lane and employed twenty four staff including cook, drill master, trade manager and two school masters in the home and teachers, door keepers and a sick visitor and a Bible woman in the mission. His hot dinners and soups were famous in Stepney. And both boys' work (the wood choppers sold wood to the value of £765) and the tract shop were 'driving a fair business'."*[100]

In 1873, the first home for girls was opened at Mossford Lodge. Later on, a new Girls' village home at Barkingside was opened in which girls would be housed in little cottages – each overseen by a 'mother'. At one stage there were about 90 cottages.

The village had its own school, a laundry and a church, with a population of over 1000 children at one time.

As was common during the Victorian era, the work of social enterprise was primarily a Christian concern. Therefore, Barnardo Homes and Schools were no exception. At this stage, it is worth pointing out that Thomas Barnardo was not only a committed Evangelical Christian, but all the vision and drive for his social enterprise was inspired by his Christian faith. Barnardo derived his values from the Bible even though the constituency that he served was a lot broader than the Christian faith.

---

100   Rose 1987. 40 http://www.infed.org.thinkers/barnardo.htm

Unfortunately, what obtains today (particularly in Britain) is to deny and ignore these milestones. We denigrate the Christian foundations most of these organizations represent. Ironically, these organizations have helped shape and define our history.

I believe it is appropriate to learn directly from the lips of the founder of the institution, an institution that was perhaps the best known social intervention crusade in the last half of the Nineteenth century. He writes,

> *"Before proceeding to detail, it may be well to set in the forefront the religious principles upon which the homes are conducted. The homes have from the beginning been conducted on definitely religious lines. They are Christian institutions, carried on in the spirit of the Gospel. They are of course Protestant, but no creed or party can claim their work exclusively for its own. Every candidate or his or her responsible guardian is plainly informed at the time of application, that these are Protestant Homes, and that no other religious instruction is afforded than such as is in accordance with the teaching of the word of God. As I could not allow any question of sect or creed to close my doors in the face of a really destitute and homeless child, and admission is in no single instance with a view to proselytism."*[101]

I wonder how much of the Christian values, ethos and beliefs of the founder are still retained today?

Without a shadow of doubt, Dr. Thomas Barnardo has left a lasting legacy on the development of social care and practice with children and young people that can never be erased. It has been said that more than 350,000 children and young people were helped by Barnardo in its first hundred years.

Today, Barnardos runs well over four hundred services across the UK. The charity works with more than 100,000 children, young people and their families each year. A staff-strength of over seven thousand run almost four hundred charity shops.

However, his focus and concern for the whole person is what I believe history will mostly remember Dr. Thomas Barnardo for. Today, Christian practice may be nothing more than mere rhetoric and telling folk what to do and to avoid.

Barnardo not only preached the Living Word to a dying generation, he further demonstrated the goodness in practice by providing education, homes and families for the most socially destitute. He also gave each person a reason to live. May God raise more people like this in our generation.

Making History

1. How do you support education initiatives in your neighbourhood (donation of books, volunteering classes, organizing events, etc)?

2. How do you support orphanages and other homes in your neighbourhood (visits, donations, networking donor agancies to support them)?

3. How much volunteer work are you engaged in through the year?

THE SPHERE OF BUSINESS – KINGDOM ENTREPRENEURS

22 *ARTHUR GUINNESS*
Entrepreneur and social reformer

|||||||||||||||||||||||||||||||| ||||||||||||||||||||||||||||||||||||||||||||||||||||||||||||||||||||||||||||||||||||

"Gin, cursed fiend, with fury fraught makes human race a prey. It enters by a deadly Draught and Steals our Life away."

Rev. James Townley (1714-1778),
English dramatist and anonymous playwright

"Drink no longer water, but use a little wine for thy stomach's sake and thine often infirmities."

(1 Timothy 5:23, KJV)

"Ye are the salt of the earth: but if the salt have lost his savour, wherewith shall it be salted? it is thenceforth good for nothing, but to be cast out, and to be trodden under foot of men.

Ye are the light of the world. A city that is set on an hill cannot be hid.

Neither do men light a candle, and put it under a bushel, but on a candlestick; and it giveth light unto all that are in the house.

Let your light so shine before men, that they may see your good works, and glorify your Father which is in heaven."

(Matthew 5:13-16, KJV)

Arthur Guinness (1725-1803) was an Irish brewer and the founder of the Guinness brewery business and family. He was an entrepreneur, visionary and philanthropist. There has been some controversy over the year of his birth. While some argue it is 1724, others point to 1725. The date he died, however, is not in doubt, the 23rd of January 1803.

In 1761 he married Olivia Whitmore in St Mary's Church, Dublin. Their union was blessed with twenty-one children, ten of whom lived up to adulthood. Arthur was born into a Protestant family who took their Christian faith seriously. His godfather was Arthur Price, Archbishop of Castel to the Church of Ireland. He was the one who bequeathed Arthur £100 in his will. This bequest was the seed money that would serve as startup capital for his business. The business would later grow to become an empire, with branches all over the world.

I have argued earlier in this book that John Wesley, the famous Revivalist of the 18th century and the founder of the Methodist Church, without doubt stands out as one of the most influential Brits of all times. This is because not only does his influence transcend the sacred and the profane, but it goes beyond geographical, cultural, economic and generational lines.

Arthur Guinness was not only a disciple but he was greatly inspired and motivated by the life and teachings of John Wesley.

John Wesley's social teaching in his day was,

> *"Make all you can, save all you can and give all you can."*

This mantra gave the upper class and the business tycoons of the day something to work with. Many of them, including Arthur Guinness, used their wealth and business as a mission project for social responsibility and Kingdom expansion.

The life of Arthur Guinness is the story of a normal, ordinary person doing extraordinary things. It is a classic example of a New Testament saint doing ministry in the market place, becoming salt and light in society. He was engaging and changing societal ills, as he made God famous in his time through his mission activities.

For so many centuries, the Church has been taught that the work done in our Cathedrals and Church buildings was sacred and holy, while that done in the secular world was ungodly and profane.

Arthur Guinness did not subscribe to such unbiblical dogma. By following the teachings of the Reformation, he learnt that all works done to the glory of God are holy and that God empowers people with a variety of gifts and talents, all to be used to glorify Him.

Social Responsibility

I have studied the life of Jesus Christ and noticed that, without exception, people always thronged and followed him wherever He went. I then asked myself the golden question: why was this so? Straight away the answer came to my heart. Whatever the need (be it social, emotional, or economic) Jesus was always concerned about people. The exception, however, was the hypocrites. He never left them the way He met them. This quality of Jesus' character is what made the life and business of Arthur Guinness stand out.

To fully understand the impact he made in his days, it is important we take a glimpse into the social milieu of his day.

In the 1600s, water flowing around the cities of Europe was nearly poisonous. In most cases, fatalities from the poisonous water were in thousands.

This was largely due to the problem of sanitation and hygiene. People did not dispose of their sewage in a hygienic manner. This unhygienic habit of sewage disposal polluted the water.

The people therefore had two options, either to drink the polluted water or to drink liquor. Around this time Parliament had banned the importation of hard liquor from Europe in the late 1600's, particularly from France. This forced people to resort to making their own gin at home. The resultant effect in England and Ireland was a steep rise in alcoholism with its attendant problems. During this period, the common phrase in front of pubs and beer houses was,

"Drunk for a penny, dead drunk for two pence and straw for nothing."

Arthur Guinness witnessed the social problem of drunkenness in Ireland for several years. He was so burdened, he earnestly wanted a change in the lot of his fellow Irish.

This burden made him cry out earnestly to God,

"God do something about the drunkenness on the streets of Ireland."

What was God's response to his prayers?

"Make a drink that men will drink that will be good for them!"

This was his life mission. No one ever fulfilled destiny or achieved purpose until they discovered their life mission.

First, Arthur Guinness' mission and mandate is a classic example of providing a social alternative. Our society today is filled with too many people who can identify the social ills, but have no solution to the problems. We have too many arm-chair critics, including Christians.

They are well-versed in the political, economic, social as well the religious malaise that plague our nation. Unfortunately, they will neither proffer a solution nor lift a finger.

Arthur Guinness' approach was quite the opposite.

Secondly, and as we have seen throughout this book, ministry cannot and should not be limited to the confines of a church building nor to certain days. Real ministry actually begins outside the four walls of a church, on a recurrent basis.

Real ministry is what takes place in society, in the slums and on the streets. Real ministry is when we change the life of the least, the last and the lost!

Thirdly, the life of Arthur Guinness debunks the age-long philosophy that you cannot be rich and also be a genuine Christian or disciple of Christ. The defence of this school of thought is rooted in the scripture which declares,

> *"...It is easier for a camel to go through the eye of a needle, than for a rich man to enter into the kingdom of God."*
>
> (Matthew 19:24, KJV)

In Arthur Guinness we see a practicing Christian making a lot of money, yet using his wealth as a change agent. This is an inspiration and a challenge to all wealthy Christians, entrepreneurs, politicians and business moguls.

So how did Arthur Guinness affect the society of his day? What practical things did he do? What legacy did he leave behind?

First, Arthur Guinness must be remembered for creating the Guinness Stout Beer as a healthy substitute for the gin craze that bedevilled our nation and the disease-infested water people drank.

It must be pointed out that the initial motive was not to set out to make as much money as possible, but to make a nutritious drink. Medical science has even attested to its nutritional and medicinal qualities. This is why the National Health Service has prescribed Guinness Stout Beer for women who are pregnant. Furthermore, the alcoholic content of the original Guinness beer was very low, making it difficult for people to get drunk easily. Thus, it could be safe to conclude that Arthur Guinness did business as a mission directive to eradicate alcoholism on the streets of Ireland.

Sometimes mission work is not restricted to travelling several thousand miles to a remote village in Africa or Asia. It might be happening in our backyard or in our street, village, town or city.

Philanthropy

Arthur Guinness was a generous giver to worthy causes, a virtue that 21st century men and women should emulate!

One day, Arthur Guinness was walking down the streets of Ireland. By divine providence, he met a young man burdened and crying about the plight of abandoned children roaming the streets.

"Why are you crying?" Arthur Guinness asked this young man. His answer was,

> *"Because of the hundreds and thousands of children roaming the streets of Ireland."*

Arthur Guinness now posed another question, "What would you do if I gave you some money?" The young man, with tears in his eyes, answered,

> *"I'd buy a home, a Christian home and we'd fill it with God's love, and we'd fill it with these children to be parented and loved in the way God intended for them to be loved."*

The young man was none other than Thomas Barnardo, the founder of the famous Barnardo homes. Arthur Guinness was one of his key financiers.

Any lessons for would-be social reformers, businessmen and women and Christians generally? I believe a lot. For one, our wealth must be seen or perceived as evidence of a calling from God.

Apart from the above, Arthur Guinness was the founder of the first Sunday School in Ireland.

At another time Arthur Guinness met a young man who wanted to become a missionary to China, but was refused by the Missionary Society. His name was Hudson Taylor.

Guinness said to this young man,

"If you are willing to go, I'll pay for you!"

Later, Hudson Taylor wrote back that more workers were needed, to which Guinness replied,

"I'll find the next ten and send them and pay for them to come!"

Eventually, Guinness saw the need to train candidates who would be sent to China as missionaries. His response to this need was to build a missionary college that would train missionaries. He demonstrated practical ways to expend ones wealth for the furtherance of God's Kingdom.

Arthur Guinness further had a deep understanding of a Christian virtue that most 21st century Christians need to learn. We are stewards of everything and owners of nothing. We are simply channels for getting the blessings across to deserving people!

Later on in life, in recognition of his enormous contribution in philanthropy, he was elevated to the House of Lords and became Lord Iveagh.

Making History

1 'Health is wealth' as the saying goes. How much of your wealth and skill are you willing to make available for people to live healthy lives?

2 Giving is a habit and attitude. What charities do you give to, no matter how little or much you make?

3 What missionary work are you committed to in terms of support or volunteering?

4 Can you identify one social problem that you can offer a solution for?

5 Identify two virtues from the life of Arthur Guinness that challenge you the most.

23 *JESSE BOOT*
Chemist to the nation

"Defend the poor and fatherless: do justice to the afflicted and needy."

(Psalm 82:3, KJV)

"The righteous considereth the cause of the poor: but the wicked regardeth not to know it."

(Proverbs 29:7, KJV)

"We declare –
For pure Drugs
For qualified assistants
For first class shops
For reasonable prices
For good health
For our moderate profits
We minister to the comfort of the community in a
*   hundred ways."*

Jesse Boot, (1850-1931) British entrepreneur

"By keeping prices down, whilst maintaining the purity and quality of what we sell, we have ensured the permanency of our trade."

Jesse Boot, 1904

"Our name has become a household word and we have many customers whose parents have dealt with our firm."

Jesse Boot, 1910

As I study the history of Great Britain, I am amazed at how much of it is dotted with such JudeoChristian heritage. It seems to me that the very foundation of British society is Christian.

What amazes me even more is the deliberate and concerted efforts of particular groups and individuals in our nation. They seek to deny, disregard or denigrate our Christian heritage.

What, however, excites me is the inspiration and lessons of history that present day Christians can imbibe from our past. These lessons, I strongly believe, are very much needed at a time when most people no longer understand or care about the welfare of their neighbour. This is one of the fundamental lessons we can learn from the life of Jesse Boot.

Jesse Boot was born on the 2nd of June 1850. He died on the 13th of June 1931.

Married to Florence Anne Rowe, his mother was Mary Wells while his father was John Boot, a farm labourer. The family lived in Hockley, an overcrowded and poor area of 19th century Nottingham.

Jesse's father, John Boot, opened a small shop selling herbal remedies. Disaster struck when John Boot suddenly died while Jesse was only ten years old.

As with most history makers who have to overcome one form of challenge or the other, Jesse not only suffered the trauma of having lost his father at a young age, he also had to abandon school at the age of thirteen. To make ends meet, he began to work in the shop.

He was a very diligent worker, serving behind the counter, preparing remedies, counting money in the till and stacking the shelves with new products.

When Jesse was 21, he became a partner in 'MARY & JESSIE BOOT HERBALIST', as the shop was then known.

What is so important to our study is Jesse's principle of social justice.

As is common today with many multi-national corporations and businesses, the established chemist in Nottingham in those days had a price-fixing policy. They out-priced most of the poor people in Nottingham who could not afford their products, thereby jeopardising their health and well-being.

Jessie Boot, a very devout Methodist, was deeply concerned about the poverty he saw in Nottingham.

Here lies the foundation and secret of this giant national retailer, concern for the consumer's welfare over and above gain and profit. This is a virtue that we 21st century Christians must imbibe in a day that mammon has taken hold of hearts and minds.

What was Jesse's business strategy? He began buying stock in bulk, embarking on aggressive advertising, and employing a bell ringer to advertise with the slogan,

"Health for a shilling!"

Jesse's policy of superior goods at competitive prices delivered with expert care meant that the *Boot* name quickly became synonymous with quality, value and service!

Boot also advertised in the Nottingham Daily Express that the 128 items in his shop at Goosedale were being sold at reduced prices.[102]

To complete his campaign Boot renamed his shop "The People's Store."

At another stage, Jesse Boot adopted another strategy to break the monopoly of the doctors.

---

102   www.spartacus.schoolnet.co.uk/Buboot.htm

During this time, doctors made up their own prescriptions after diagnosing what was wrong with their patients. The cost of the prescriptions was so high that this often stopped the poor patients from receiving the much needed treatment they deserved.

Boot decided to break this monopoly by employing a certain E. S. Waring, a young chemist, to provide prescriptions.

It was said that, on average, the cost of these prescriptions was less than half of those charged by the doctors.[103]

The cumulative effect of all these was an increase in patronage, higher profits, greater and wider publicity for the business.

This is a great lesson for all of us today, particularly those of us living in an age where greed rules.

The interest of customers must always come first before profit. Anytime customer relations management is geared towards the benefit of the customer, profits are bound to skyrocket, as we have seen from the story of Boots the Chemist.

Boots the Chemist at the early stage was not only interested in selling medicines, but they were also concerned with the people's diet.

We all know the age-old saying, "You are what you eat".

It has been proven over the years that our diet is a key factor to our state of health. In this sense, Boots the Chemist were forerunners in teaching people how to cook and eat good food.

At one stage, they ran little cookery classes and later added household utensils, like pots and pans, to what they sold.

---

103 www.spartacus.schoolnet.co.uk/Buboot.htm

Workers' Welfare

> *"Woe unto him that buildeth his house by unrighteousness, and his chambers by wrong; that useth his neighbour's service without wages, and giveth him not for his work;"*
>
> (Jeremiah 22:13, KJV)

One of the fundamental vices that the prophets of old denounced during their days was the problem of fat cats not paying their workers wages commensurate with their labour.

It appears not much has changed since then if we look critically at the business models of our present day multinationals and business concerns.

Jesse Boot and the Boot Company were forerunners in putting workers' welfare before company profits.

To Jesse and Florence, the wellbeing of their employees was paramount. They provided welfare, education, sports and social facilities for their growing retail and manufacturing workforce. Full time welfare professionals were employed and a surgery was established at the Island Street site to care for the healthcare needs of employees. In the field of education, Jesse opened a Day Continuation School (later renamed Boots College) which was opened to provide extended academic and vocational education for younger employees.

Jesse and Florence were not employers who stood aloof from their workers. They understood the importance of connecting with their staff. From time to time they hosted social events, outings for staff such as trips to the sea-side and musical concerts. They also helped fund and establish numerous societies, sporting and social clubs with the belief that healthy and happy employees would make their business a happy and productive place to work.

The following statement by Jesse Boot helps bring this point home.

He remarked, "We are primarily comrades – and close comrades, moreover in business and this is no mean tie, for business, claiming as it does so much of our time and talents, is a highly important feature in our lives .... If our labour is nothing to us but a means of procuring bread and butter then our lives must be a poor thankless round of dull task work..... While we are primarily business associates, our mutual interests are by no means restricted to business in any limited sense. Fellowship in recreation, fellowship in ideals, common hopes, common sympathies and common humanity bind us together, and whatever fosters this happy union is valuable"[104]

Promotion Of Medical Science

The place of knowledge in the development of any given society cannot be overemphasized.

Jesse Boot was not only satisfied with helping people, he believed in empowering them. To this end, he made great contributions to the establishment of Nottingham University, particularly with the vision of making affordable medicines available for the populace. Even today, the University of Nottingham publicly acknowledges on their website the pivotal role that Jesse Boot made to the founding of the institution.

"Philanthropy played a fundamental role in establishing the University of Nottingham. Sir Jesse Boot's generosity in providing land and buildings to fund the University was a turning point for the institution..."[105]

104 Jesse Boot 1919, www.boots_uk.com/AboutBoots/Boots_Heritage/Boots-Histo-ryaspx
105 www.globalviewnottingham.uk/university

Jesse Boot also promoted education in another way. When the business commenced cookery classes, they discovered a high percentage of attendees were illiterate.

How did they respond? They began to help people to read and write, adding books to their shelves and running a book lending scheme. This was a fore-runner of the British Library Lending System.

So successful did Boots the Chemist grow that by 1933 it opened its 1,000th Boots Store, in Galashiels, Scotland.

For his various contributions to Nottingham and the nation at large, Jesse Boot was knighted in 1909. He thus became Sir Jesse Boot.

The life and story of Jesse Boot epitomizes the triumph of victory over adversity. The iron-clad will of a Christian man took seriously his vocation and calling in the market place to make his society a better place. My prayer is that God will stir up the likes of Jesse Boot to be light and salt in this degenerating generation.

Making History

1. Jesse Boot was an example par excellence in social justice. In what practical ways can you champion social justice in your community or nation?

2. As a business person can you identify with him to leave a lasting legacy?

3. What is the greatest lesson that you learnt from the life of Jesse Boot and how do you intend to incorporate this into your life, business or ministry?

THE SPHERE OF MEDIA

"The Lord gave the word; great was the company that published it"

(Psalm 68:11 KJV)

No right thinking individual or government will ever undermine the power of the media! So powerful is the modern day media that it has not only been rightly described as the fourth arm of government, but has been responsible for the raising and dethroning of governments, kings, potentates, businesses and corporations as well as individuals!

Today the British media is dominated by Rupert Murdoch, his ever increasing empire, and his allies characterised by obscene, pornographic, violent, God mocking, Jesus dishonouring materials and programmes. With a high percentage of children and young ones who are computer literate – pornographic materials are just a click away to anyone including children as young as four years old.

Unfortunately most of the owners of these media outfits, with the support of some politicians, see nothing wrong with this!

As a responsible father, I am ever apprehensive about my children not stumbling across some of the explicit sexual programmes beamed everyday even on mainstream television.

Any casual looker or visitor to Britain might conclude that the present despicable, distasteful and disgraceful programming that mostly characterise our broadcasting has always been like this! You would grossly be in error.

CHAPTER 24

THE BBC AND LORD REITH

Through my study and research, I have argued over the last two decades that many of the iconic institutions in Britain had a spiritual vision behind them. Their origins were born out of faith, by this, I mean the Christian faith! The British Broadcasting Corporation is a classic example!

What I am about to write next will shock many people across the world, particularly those who are fed up or disgusted by the horrific, violent, obscene and pornographic programmes that have characterized television broadcasting in our nation!

Did you know that when the BBC, the first world broadcasting organisation, was founded in 1927, it adopted as its vision statement "Nation shall speak peace unto nation", which it claimed was inspired by the phrase in the Bible. The Prophet Micah wrote: "Nation shall not lift up sword against nation; neither shall they learn war anymore."

Furthermore, in 1934, a new official motto was adopted for 15 years before reverting to the original. This time the motto was "Quaecunque", the Latin word for "whatsoever", this time inspired from the Bible – Philippians 4:8.

"Finally, brethren, whatsoever things are true, whatsoever things are honest, whatsoever things are just, whatsoever things are pure, whatsoever things are lovely, whatsoever things are of good report; if there be any virtue, and if there be any praise, think on these things."

In the dedication of the BBC Broadcasting House headquarters in London, opened in 1931, the entrance hall embodies the inscription, which translates "To Almighty God. This shrine of the arts, music and literature is dedicated by the first governors in the year of our Lord 1931, John Reith being director general. It is their prayer that good seed sown will produce a good harvest, that everything offensive to decency and hostile to peace will be expelled and that the nation will incline its ear to those things which are lovely, pure and of good report and thus pursue the path of wisdom and virtue."

No doubt, anyone who is conversant with the history of the BBC would agree that it would not be what it is today without the input, inspiration and exemplary leadership of its first Director General – Lord Reith. He was himself a committed Christian, whose Christian faith permeated most things he did at the corporation!

Born on the 20th of July 1889 at Storehaven, Kincarchinshire to George Reith, who was himself a minister in the Free Church of Scotland, his own brother Archie was also a Church of England Vicar in Norfolk. All this shows deep family roots in the Christian faith.

He was a man who strongly believed in the efficacy of prayer. On his preparation for his interview for the BBC job, he did nothing other than pray! Indeed his prayers were answered when on the next day of his interview he was offered the job at the BBC for £1,750 a year.

John Reith was a man of deep spiritual conviction – a trait that is mostly lacking among many Christians in the public arena today! John Reith's Christian convictions were displayed while at the BBC in the famous Eckersley affair – his chief engineer in 1929, who was sacked for having an extra-marital affair.

One BBC interviewee in the 1920's remembers being asked by the Director General "Do you accept the fundamental teachings of Jesus Christ?"

Peter Eckersley, in his memoirs, makes a profound statement about his dismissal by his boss-John Reith. "I happened to come under the control of that rare individual who acts according to his spiritual convictions."[106]

Perhaps the most outstanding achievement or legacy that John Reith not only bequeathed to the BBC, the media world, Britain and indeed the world at large was the Empire Service, which later became known as the World Service! This commenced broadcast in 1932. One will only appreciate the importance of the World Service if we understand that for several million across the world – as far as remote villages in Africa and Asia and for many decades – their only source of reliable and efficient news was the BBC World Service. Little wonder that the former UN Secretary General Kofi Annan once described the BBC World-Service as "Britain's greatest gift to the world in the 20th century"[107]. Really what Kofi Annan describes as Britain's gift to the world was actually the brainchild of John Reith.

The big challenge today is for Christians with deep spiritual convictions rooted in Scripture to arise and take their place in this sphere as John Reith did!

It must be said that a lot has been achieved in the last twenty years in Christian media – even though it can be said that we are barely scratching the surface.

As I have often remarked-one of the greatest mistakes we can make as Christians is to neglect or ignore this sphere of the society. Whether we like it or not, the media is perhaps the greatest tool of influence in any nation. All you need to consider is the impact that the media has on our children, the next generation – from music, to fashion, to films or sports. All our children are influenced by the power of the media! From their shoes, to their choice of music to football hero – everything is conditioned by the power of the media!

....

106   http://www.bbc.co.uk/history of the bbc/resources/in-depth
107   Source: www.bbc.co.uk/historyofthebbc/resources

25 *J. ARTHUR RANK*
The film industry
pioneer and reformer

Before ending this chapter, it is worth mentioning that, apart from John Reith, there are several other Christians who have influenced the media in Britain. Time and space will not permit me to mention all of them, but it's worth mentioning in passing the work of J. Arthur Rank (22nd December 1888 to 29th March 1972) because of his impact in the film industry.

He was born on the 23rd of December 1888 in Kingston Upon Hull in England into a Victorian family environment, which was dominated by his father Joseph Rank who had built a substantial flour milling business.

Arthur Rank came from a deeply religious family, with their roots in the Methodist Church. During his mid-life he taught Sunday School and began to show religious films, first in his local church and later to other churches and schools. This eventually led to his formation of the religious film society to which he then distributed films that he had made!

J. Arthur Rank was both a pioneer and a reformer in the film industry in Britain. When the Methodist Times began to complain about the negative influence that British and American films shown in Britain were having on family life, their editorial was answered by the London Evening News who suggested that instead of complaining the Methodist Church should provide a solution.

True reformers don't just identify a problem, they offer solutions! What use is a medical doctor who simply diagnoses an ailment but cannot bring a cure? J. Arthur Rank was not a man given to the status-quo. He would not leave things the way he found them! He had two options − to ignore the damage caused to family life and society from the influence of unwholesome films or to reform things! He chose the latter, for he took up the challenge and via an introduction by a young film producer − John Cornfield and Lady Yule of Bricket Wood, he discussed both the problem and the solution. The result was the formation of the British National Film Company.

Perhaps the greatest legacy that J. Arthur Rank left to the British film industry was that he produced films that had wholesome values and principles. He had a company policy which he solidly kept to inspite of American challenges and competition, which was to produce "family − friendly" films.

To this end in 1953 he set up the J. Arthur Rank Group charity to promote Christian belief!

If there was a time that we need both men and women who will be reformers in the film industry, it is now!

Never before has any generation experienced large scale perversion, violence and corruption in what is taking place in our film industry! The call is loud and clear − Who shall I send and who will go for us? I believe one of the reasons for writing this book is to wake up the sleeping giant. I hope you are not just being educated but also inspired and challenged! As Christians we must stop complaining about the horrific, pornographic and violent films being shown in our homes and cinemas, if we are not prepared to challenge and change the status-quo by offering our families high quality, interesting but family friendly and God honouring films.

To appreciate the contribution of J. Arthur Rank to the British film industry, one only needs to realise that during the 1940s the companies that Rank controlled produced some of the finest British films of the period, which include *The Life and Death of Colonel Blimp* (1943), *Henry V* (1944), *A Matter of Life and Death* (1946), *Black Narassus* (1947), and *The Red Shoes* (1948).[108]

Furthermore, in 1935, Rank with two others – Lady Yule and John Cornfield were to acquire the Pinewood Film Studios to rival Hollywood in California. Later Lady Yule sold her shares to Rank, while John Cornfield resigned from its board of directors.

Apart from consolidating his film production interests, both in Pinewood Film Studio and the Denham Film Studios, in 1938 he bought the Odeon cinema chain and the Amalgamated Studios in Elstree. In 1941 it absorbed the Gaumont, which owned 251 cinemas, and the Lime Grove studios (later owned by the BBC) and bought the Paramount Cinema chain, so that by 1942 the Rank Organisation owned 619 cinemas. This shows the extent of Rank's influence in the film industry in Britain! The prayer of many today is that God will raise many more Christians like J Arthur Rank, who will be salt and light in a dark and decadent sphere of our society!

---

108   Source https;/en.wikipedia.org/wiki.J-Arthur-Rank,_1st baron_rank

Making History

1. How strategic do you think the media is in any nation?
2. Can you highlight some things or issues that infuriate you in the secular media and what strategies do you think we can adopt to change things?
3. "Evil will continue when righteous people refuse to act." How applicable is this to the present state of the BBC?
4. What lessons can you learn from the life of J. Arthur Rank?
5. What do you think the church, pastors and church leaders should be doing to encourage Christians in the media sphere?

THE SPHERE OF CELEBRATION

26 *ISAAC WATTS The father of English hymns*

||||||||||||||||||||||||||||||| |||||||||||||||||||||||||||||||||||||||||||||||||||||||||||||||||||||||||||||||||||||||

"Give yourselves to God...Surrender your whole being to Him to be used for righteous purposes."
(Romans 6:13, Today's English Version)

"In the same way that you gave me a mission in the world, I give them a mission in the world."
(John 17:18)

The Message

The history of Britain and indeed that of the Church cannot be written without the contributions of the hymn writers. When it comes to the best known, most sought-after hymns that inspired both men and kings, Britain gave them to the world.

Isaac Watts

Without controversy, Isaac Watts (1674-1748) is regarded as the "Father of English hymnody". He was perhaps the most gifted man that England has ever given to the Church. His poetic gift was already evident at the tender age of seven.

At the time of his death in 1748, he had written more than 700 hymns, most of which are regularly sung in services of Christian worship.

Many people are aware of the outstanding revival that God sent through the hands of the duo, John Wesley and George Whitefield. However, only few are aware of Isaac Watts' contribution.

What John the Baptist was to Jesus' ministry, so Isaac Watts was to the Revivalists whom God used to bring about the Great Awakening.

The spiritual climate in England during the 18th century was characterised by mere formality, dead orthodoxy, apathy and indifference. There was great darkness over the land and gross darkness over the people. It was at this strategic moment that God stirred up Isaac Watts to lead England and America to a spiritual awakening through the instrument of hymns. Interestingly, hymns were very much unknown in his day.

His Beginnings

Isaac Watts is someone who can best be referred to as a reformer. Unlike our days when people are mostly critical of what they perceive as being wrong or need to change, Isaac Watts identified a need in the Church and would not let things continue in the status quo. He took a stand. Let's see how he came to be the best hymn-writer of all time.

Gene Fedele, in his book *Heroes Of The Faith* writes:

> *"It was immediately after his academy days, when he had returned to live in his father's home, that Watts composed his first hymn. One Sunday after the morning church service he began to complain about the dull and lifeless psalm – singing in which they had just participated, a characteristic of nonconformist worship at that time. The elder Watts replied, "if you do not*

like it, why do you not give us something better?" Isaac went home, opened his bible to a place in Revelation, Chapter 5 where the New Song of Heaven is described and wrote a poetic transcription of it. Two of the stanzas read:

Behold the glories of the lamb
Amid Father's throne
Prepare new honours for his name
And songs before unknown
Thou hast redeemed our souls with blood
Hast set the prisoners free
Hast made us kings and priests to God
And we shall reign with thee.[109]

Gene Fedele continues,

"This first effort was sung at the next service in the Southampton church. It touched the hearts of those in the congregation and moved them so deeply they encouraged him to write songs for them. So on that day, the English hymn was born."[110]

One of the greatest lessons I strongly believe the Church of the 21st century must learn and glean from the life of Isaac Watts and many hymn-writers is that their songs were deeply rooted in Scripture. Isaac Watts made it possible, like the psalmist, for God's people to sing from God's Word. Unlike some musicians today, Isaac Watts highly honoured the Word of God. I believe this disposition of his in itself was deeply rooted in his spiritual standing with his Saviour. I have often wondered at how many of the hymns written about 300 years ago are still being sung today and are refreshingly inspirational.

---

109 *Heroes of The Faith*, Gene Fedele, Bridge Logos, Florida, 2003
110 Ibid, p 155

So great was the effect of Isaac Watt's hymns on people during his life time that Rev. Philip Doddridge, in a letter to Watts, mentioned a church service at which the congregation sang "Give Me The Wings Of Faith To Rise Within The Veil".

Doddridge wrote,

> *"I had the satisfaction to observe tears in the eyes of several of the people and after the service was over some of them told me they were not able to sing because their hearts were so deeply affected. They were most of them poor people who worked for their living; yet at the mention of your name, I found.......that your psalms and hymns were almost their daily entertainment."*[111]

I believe the mantle of men like Isaac Watts is waiting to be picked up by men and women who are jealous for the glory of God and those who would love God to be famous once again not only in the British Church, but all over our nation and indeed the world at large!

As you read this, ponder on this question: could God be calling you into the sphere of celebration? Is He calling you to write and sing songs that will honour, glorify Him, inspire and edify both men and kings?

Some of Isaac Watts' most popular hymns include *O God Our Help In Ages Past, Before Jehovah's Throne, Joy To The World, Come Holy Spirit and When I Survey The Wondrous Cross!*

---

111   Ibid, p 158

Making History

1. Like the father of English hymns, can you identify something in your community, church, or nation that you can change or reform?

2. Writing is not limited to songs; it can be uplifting poems, stories and articles. What platforms are you exploiting to reach out to those who need some comfort for their spirit and soul?

3. Your gift is meant to be an inspiration to others. How connected are you to God for inspiration, through His Word, the Bible?

27 *CHRISTIANITY AND THE GAME OF FOOTBALL*

"Soccer was 'a grand game' for developing a lad physically and also morally, for he learns to play with good temper and unselfishness, to play in his place and 'play the game', and these are the best of training for any game of life."

Robert Baden-Powell OM, GCMG, GCVO, KCB (1857-1941),
Founder of the Boy Scouts, 1908

"I know why logs split. I know what it is to be consumed on sitting by a fireplace and staring into the flames."

Winston Leonard Spencer Churchill (1874-1965),
Prime Minister of the United Kingdom

I have included this chapter in this book for a number of reasons.

Firstly, because of how important the game of football is to the British people and indeed the world at large. Only few people today will argue about the unequalled status that football holds in the sporting arena.

Secondly, I intend to highlight the role football has played in social reform and the lessons that we can learn today for doing Christian mission.

Finally, this chapter is meant to help set the record straight about the origins and the development of our national game, football.

217

In my first book, *Great Britain Has Fallen*, I argued from reliable historical sources that the foundation and the very fabric of the British society are completely Christian. The footprints of Christianity span everywhere. Christianity etched an indelible mark on our society which cannot be erased.

The game of football, popularly referred to as the King of Sports, is not an exception.

The Origins Of The Game

Before I go into the origins of football in our nation, I believe it's worth stating an immutable fact. Of the thirty-nine clubs that played in the English Football Association Premier League since its inception in the 1992-93 season, twelve of them owe their existence to churches. Unfortunately, most of the supporters of these great clubs (and I even suspect, some of the players) are ignorant of these facts.

The history of football will be incomplete without mention being made of the 19th century Sunday School Movement. So popular was the Sunday School Movement, it is estimated that about 85% of children in our nation attended regularly.

My sincere prayer is that God will return us to those days again. During these times, the Church engaged the communities around them. The origins of football could be traced to the Churches' response to a dire need in society among children and young people.

As the number of young people increased to record levels, there was a need to provide activities for children and young ones in order to divert their minds from alcohol, sex and crime. It seems to me, as I read the pages of history, that history seems to be repeated.

The same social milieu prevalent today is similar to what obtained in the 19th century. The only question is this: are we learning any lessons? Can we respond appropriately to the social challenges of our days?

On the origins of football in Britain, Dave Roberts in an article *Aston Villa and the Mission of God* remarks,

"Outside of the context of Sunday, the church was the main provider of activity for children and young people whose numbers in the society were at record level. As people moved from agriculture based existence towards living in the most basic of accommodation in large cities, they often sought solace in a 'third place'. That was usually the public house. The vicars, priests and ministers who helped pioneer these new sporting diversions were deeply averse to the idea of sport on Sunday. They also had a very distinct temperance agenda.

With the advent of the five and a half-day week, Saturday afternoon drunkenness was becoming a problem. The 3.00pm kick off was partly a result of the desire of the church leaders to keep men from spending an afternoon drinking their wages away!"[112]

It is worth mentioning at this stage that Peter Lupson has done not only the Church a great service, but our nation. In addition, his service further extends to all those interested in discovering the origins of this game in Britain.

According to him, we cannot speak of the origins without tracing it back to the Church, particularly the Wesleyan Methodist Church. Reflecting on the beginning of the Aston Villa Football Club in his book, "Thank God for Football" he writes,

"Aston Villa" was originally the name of a large mansion that stood virtually opposite the chapel in the Aston District of Birmingham at the junction of Heathfield Road and Lozella Road. The building was a significant landmark and gives its name to the immediate locality and it is from the Aston Villa locality that the chapel derives its name.

----

112 *Aston Villa and the Mission of God*, Dave Roberts, Christianity Magazine, June 2010 Edition, p 35

The chapel attached great importance to its work with young people and when two houses adjoining it were bought in 1871, the one closest was fitted out with classrooms to help cater for the over 300 young people who attended the Sunday School. These were grouped according to age and gender and were given instruction in the essentials of the Christian faith. One of the classes – the Young Men's Bible Class – was the cradle of Aston Villa Football Club.[113]

All this occurred in 1865. Did you notice from the above account that Aston Villa Football Club started from a Bible class? I wish I could go on the house tops and shout this to all football-loving people in Britain.

The four original founders of the club were Jack Hughes, Frederick Matthews, Walter Price and William Scattergood.

Rev. Charles Beecroft – First President

It must be placed on record that the first President of the club appointed in 1887 was a Methodist Minister, Reverend Charles Beecroft. This, I am sure, will not be conceivable to the 21st century mind that will think sports and religion cannot go together. This is a lesson for those of us serving as ministers of the Gospel today. Our forebears did not conceive of any demarcation between sport and Christianity. In fact, they believed that everything was created by God and it could and should be used to expand His Kingdom.

William McGregor – The Foundation Layer

The name that is most associated with laying a lasting foundation for what Aston Villa is today is none other than

---

113   *Thank God for Football*, pp 1-2, Azure, London, 2006

William McGregor. He was a visionary and energetic leader. In 1877, Charles Beecroft became the first President of the club. In that same year, William McGregor became a member of the club's committee at the age of 31 years. It has been said he was reputed to have helped make Aston Villa one of the most successful and prestigious clubs in the country. I am almost certain that most Aston Villa supporters are oblivious of the fact that the Scottish national symbol of a lion rampant was adopted as the club's badge because the sports enthusiast suggested it.

His contributions to the game bear greater significance on a national scale; he was the creator of the Football League. What is more important for many in this country is the fact that McGregor was a committed Christian, widely respected for his honesty and integrity.

The Reverend W. G. Percival, pastor at the Congregational Church in Wheeler Street where McGregor worshipped for over 40 years, testified about his character and Christian commitment, when he remarked that the best thing about him..., "was not so much the genial, kindly, honest sportsman, but it was the Christian behind it all".[114] He commented further that he was a man of absolutely unblemished personal character.

I really do hope that all the present Board members, coaching staff, supporters of Aston Villa, both in Britain and abroad, will take notice and be thankful for the life and contribution of William McGregor.

Barnsley Football Club and Tiverton Preedy

Tiverton Preedy was born on the 22nd of January 1863 to Charles and his wife, Mary Preedy. He was the second of four

---

114   *Thank God for Football*, Peter Lupson, pp 8-9, Azure, London, 2006

children. In 1885, at the age of 22, he gained admission into Lincoln Theological College to train for the Anglican Ministry. This was in response to a conviction he felt was a calling to service to the poor, deprived and destitute. This man would be significantly influenced by the sporting ethos of the school. I have always argued that a man's destiny can mostly be affected by his association or impartation. Be careful who you associate with. It was at the Theological College founded by one Edward Benson in 1874 in Lincoln that Tiverton Preedy caught the vision of sports as a moral agent. He embraced this muscular Christian notion with great enthusiasm. In the words of Peter Lupson,

"Little did he know what significance this would have for the Yorkshire mining town of Barnsley."[115]

1887 was a significant year in the life of Mr. Preedy. He was ordained a deacon (the same year of Queen Victoria's Golden Jubilee). The following year, he was ordained a priest.

How did Barnsley Football Club come to be formed, someone might enquire? In an interview with the *Church Times* in 1926, Rev. Preedy explained that, during his settling-in period, he joined the Barnsley Rugby Club in order to actualize his desire to connect with the community through sport.

However, his stay was to be short-lived because he soon left in protest. His club, which had hitherto always played on Saturdays, now decided to play on Good Friday, the day his Lord was crucified!

Anyone who believes in the Scriptures that declare *"All things work together for good to them that love God"* (Romans 8:28) will almost certainly concede that this move was divine.

As he walked down the street, away from the club, he came upon some young folk in front of a public house by chance. They were discussing how they would love to form a new soccer club.

115   Ibid, p 16

Preedy was not only going to join in their conversation, his vision and passion would make a great impact on these young lads. Before long the unanimous verdict was arrived at; Mr. Preedy was the man to lead the club. And so it was, Barnsley St. Peter Football Club was born.

To demonstrate the significant contributions and in honour of the founder of the club, Peter Lupson shares in his book how important the year 1912 was to the history of the club. It was the year that the club tasted national glory by winning the F.A. Cup for the first and only time in its history. The game was against West Bromwich Albion. According to accounts, the ball from that historic victory, the club's most treasured possession, was proudly displayed in the study of a Church of England Minister in Islington, London until his death in 1928.

How did this come about? Shouldn't the ball have been kept in Barnsley rather than London? Again, Peter Lupson writes,

"Simply because in the euphoria of victory, the club remembered the man to whom it owed its very existence. By presenting the cup final ball to the Reverend Tiverton Preedy immediately after the match, Barnsley Football Club was honouring its founder."[116]

Everton And Liverpool Football Clubs

Everton and Liverpool football clubs both share an interesting history. Just like other clubs mentioned, the fans are likely oblivious of such remarkable history. Both clubs owe their beginnings to one man, Reverend Benjamin Swift Chambers. In July 1887, he became the minister of a Methodist church, St Domingo Chapel.

116   Ibid, p 15

The Methodist New Connexion Conference minutes of 1902 describes him as,

> *"...a powerful and winning personality and people found themselves easily drawn to him. He was considered to be a manly, affectionate, kindly, pleasant, happy, noble being........eager to serve, anxious to do good.....a never failing friend."[117]*

Again, we see the impact both ministries of John Wesley and Methodist Church had on our national life, including the game of football.

All available records reveal that Rev. Benjamin Swift formed Everton Football Club in 1878 from the Cricket Club. The major ojective was to keep the young men of the church active during winter months. These periods were outside the cricket season.

The first home ground of Everton was at the corner of Priory Road and Arkle Lane. An important personality, who would leave a lasting impact on the history of the club, was none other than Mr. John Houlding. He became Everton's first-ever President before the start of the 1881-82 football season.

He was a very successful businessman in the brewing industry and an active politician; he was elected to represent both Everton and Kirkdale Wards in the City Council. Later, in 1897, he became Mayor of Liverpool.

During his tenure as President, Everton Football Club would move from Priory Road to Anfield, which today is home to Liverpool Football Club!

The important point in our study of both clubs is the link between them. Liverpool Football Club was founded following a dispute between the Everton Committee and John Houlding, Club President and owner of the land at Anfield. After eight years at the stadium, Everton relocated to Goodison Park

---

117   Ibid, p 58

in 1892 and Houlding founded Liverpool F.C. Anfield would become their home ground.

Originally Liverpool F.C. was called The Everton Football Club and Athletic Ground Company Limited. However, both names were denied registration by the Football Association because of a protest. The protest hinged on the similarity of the names. The protests emanated from Mr. George Maton and the Everton Governing Committee.

Once the names were denied, Mr Houlding came up with another name. This time, the name was duly registered in May 1892 as the Liverpool Association Football Clubs. Anfield Stadium is a venue that has become famous throughout the whole world today. It was actually built by Everton Football Club.

Without doubt, two of the greatest clubs in English football owe their origin to the Church. May I also add that Liverpool Football Club is perhaps the most successful club ever in English history with thirty three titles to their credit, eighteen League titles, seven F.A. Cups and eight League Cups.

Liverpool has also won more European titles than any other English club; five European Cups, three UEFA Cups and three UEFA Super Cups.

Indeed, with such outstanding achievements of the club coupled with the popularity and the influence she has earned, we cannot but join Peter Lupson in declaring,

"...Thank God for football!"

An Interesting Club

Time and space will not permit me to detail the origins and the personalities of other English clubs that had a Christian heritage. These clubs include Birmingham City, Bolton Wanderers, Fulham (2010 UEFA Cup finalists), Queens Park Rangers (promoted to the Premiership in 2012), Southampton, Swindon Town and Tottenham Hotspur.

All these football clubs not only trace their origins to the Church and Christian leaders but their influence and contributions to our national game have been unprecedented.

However, there is a club that I believe the story of its beginning is worth telling for several reasons. Firstly, this club was started in response to various social problems in society. Some of these problems included drunkenness, and street warfare coupled with serious poverty. This was around 1870-1880.

Secondly, this club today is one of the most famous clubs in the world. It definitely belongs to the league of the richest clubs in the world.

However, what has captivated me the most is the next point. Of all the famous football clubs founded by churches, individuals or organisations, only one can claim to owe its origin to the initiative of a woman. The club is Manchester City Football Club.

I am absolutely sure that this will come as a shock to most football lovers in and outside of Great Britain. It was a remarkable energetic woman, Anna Connell. A clergyman's daughter, she took the first important step that would result in the creation of a club ranked among great football clubs in England and indeed, the world, Manchester City (Premiership Champions, 2011/2012 season).

How did it all start? As mentioned earlier, the social conditions of West Gorton, then a suburb of Manchester in the 1880s, were appalling.

Poverty, sub-standard living conditions, drunkenness and street warfare were rife. Could there have been a way out of this mess? Was there an alternative? Anna Connell believed so.

She was not a woman given to leaving things in the status quo. Like most reformers, she believed that something could be done. Even though she was a woman in the 19th century, she was not going to bow down to voices that a woman's place was in the kitchen, when her community was being overtaken with evil.

How did she respond? She sought for social alternatives to the evils of her society. In practical terms, she started a working men's meeting at St. Mark's Church, West Gorton, in 1879. With her father's full support, Anna set up a programme of spiritually edifying talks and wholesome entertainment, consisting of musical evenings, concerts, singing, drama, reading and recitations.[118]

It was out of these Tuesday meetings that Anna Connell started Manchester City Football Club. This is where the club found its origin.

One thing is worth mentioning. Winners never quit and quitters never win. Great men and women who changed the course of history are never quitters. Anna Connell was a woman never given to quitting in spite of apparent insurmountable challenges. She was faced with serious setbacks but her dedication and persistence won the day. Is it any surprise to us that the club she helped pioneer fought gallantly till the very last kick of the ball to win the 2011-2012 Premiership League trophy? By this victory they edged to second place their arch rivals, Manchester United.

Is there any lesson for women, church leaders, social reformers and the Church at large? I think so.

Challenge For The 21st century Church

In view of the lessons that we have gleaned from history, particularly from Christian men and women who were pioneers of the game of football in Britain, I believe there is a big challenge for church leaders, elders and Christians generally. Christians in the 19th century were able to respond to the social challenges of their day by creating a platform to engage their communities! Today there are even more social problems that families and governments have no answers for!

118   Ibid, p 93

Without any doubt in my heart, I strongly believe the Church should get more involved in sports, particularly the game of football.

Are you aware that there is no game in the world that unites the world more than the game of football?

It unites people across national, racial, religious, economic, and social boundaries. I have seen folk, who would usually not have anything to do with each other, strike up a conversation. Such conversations last for hours as they watch a game live.

I believe the passion for football globally today has created a natural platform for Christians and churches to get involved in their communities.

Could churches not encourage or take advantage of many professional footballers who are committed Christians, who have played at the highest level in Europe and their national team to set up local football clubs in their areas? These celebrities, who are also influencers, can reach out to and engage the younger generation! So many names immediately come to mind, both from Europe, Africa and South America.

Similarly, there are other games that have a strong followership apart from football. They include lawn and table tennis, swimming, and athletics, to mention a few. These games can be used as tools to reach our communities and nations. After all, everything was created by God and should be used for His glory!

In my opinion, the sphere of celebration (which incorporates sports, music, entertainment and fashion) ranks as the most strategic in reaching our youth, the next generation.

Could this be the reason we are losing our youth to drugs, sexual urges, and violence as we have turned our back on this sphere of society? I am yet to discover a young person who is not interested in any sport, fashion, music or entertainment.

May I further add that one church I have seen engaging its community in this sphere is the Embassy of God in Ukraine led by Pastor Sunday Adelaja. If we are going to take seriously our mandate to fill the whole earth with the knowledge of the glory of the Lord, subdue the kingdom of this world and bring back the King, we must begin to take practical steps in engaging our communities and nations in the celebration sphere!

Permit me to end this chapter by stating, as I have repeated in several places for over two decades, that Christianity has lost a lot of ground in my nation of adoption, Britain. No doubt this ground needs to be recovered. This is one of my primary reasons for writing this book; to unearth our rich Judeo-Christian heritage that has been buried out of sight by either neglect or a concerted plot of those who subscribe to a humanist agenda. It's time to rise up and be counted. It's time for the Church Militant to confront the social evils of our day by providing social alternatives like our predecessors did and bring about radical transformation of our society which will bring glory and honour to our God.

Making History

1 What sustainable youth programs can you initiate in your community?

2 How much of your skill are you willing to volunteer towards mentoring young ones in your neighbourhood?

3 Which role models, aside from yourself, can you recommend as you channel the minds of young people to be responsible individuals?

4 As a pastor, elder or Board member, if the world's best footballer today were to join your ministry – how would you groom him for ministry – as an usher, choir member, pastor or as a minister and mentor in the field or sphere of sport?

REFORMATION IN REVERSE

Chapter 28
Lessons from Alice Bailey

28 *LESSONS FROM ALICE BAILEY*

||||||||||||||||||||||||||||||||||| ||||||||||||||||||||||||||||||||||||||||||||||||||||||||||||||||||||||||||||||||||||

"Subtlety may deceive you; integrity never will."
Oliver Cromwell (1599-1658),
English military and political leader

"The essence of lying is in deception, not in words."
John Ruskin (1819-1900),
English art critic and prominent social thinker

*"Knowledge of God's Word is a bulwark against
deception, temptation, accusation, even persecution."*
Edwin Louis Cole (1922-2002),
Founder of the Christian Men's Network

We have seen individuals who have etched their names in the annals of Great Britain's history. Their exploits have been phenomenal in their respective endeavours and have become legacies we enjoy today.

However, I introduce yet another individual but whose legacy has a rather unnerving twist to it.

Few people know of Alice Bailey and even fewer know anything about the impact that she had on Great Britain, the Western World and indeed the world at large. Any serious student of history will know that apart from the Middle

East, which is the cradle of Christianity, no other part of the globe has felt the impact of Christianity in society more than Western Europe.

Take a look, for example, at Great Britain and consider the impact that Christianity has had in her history as a nation.

In my first book *Great Britain Has Fallen* I argued that the history of Great Britain would be incomplete in the last 1500 years without mention being made of the impact Christianity has had on the British Society. I quoted Libby Purves, a regular contributor to Times Newspaper (30th November 1999), reflecting on the present state of Christianity. She wrote,

> *"Even atheists should be interested, for Christianity touches everybody every day. In the past thousand years it has been by far the largest single influence on culture, institutions, laws, education and the structure of society in these islands. The Book of Common Prayer and the Authorized Version hover over our literature, our lawyers and academics are clerically robed, our law enshrines commandments (modern compensation law depends on the "neighbor principle" drawn from the second line of Moses tablet)."*
>
> *The Reformation, a dramatic dislocation of daily life and intimate customs, fuelled both a powerful stream of questing English intellectualism and I suspect the national vice of nostalgia, the dream of a past different and better, tenderer and more ornate. Neo-classicism would not have happened without the clerical and therefore educational bias towards the scriptural languages; in politics our House of Commons sits in two opposing parties rather than a semi circle merely because they started out in chapel choir stalls. It has even been persuasively argued that Anglophones would never have been world leaders in pop lyrics and*

> *musicals were not that we were taught to combine*
> *tune, sense and emotion by the great 19th century*
> *Wesley hymns and to give the result a swing by the*
> *incoming black gospel tradition. Like it or loathe it*
> *Christianity leaves great footprints over every aspect of*
> *national life."[119]*

My submission in this book is that the very foundation and fabric of British society is completely Christian. I further argued that the greatness and prosperity that our nation has enjoyed over the centuries have been as a result of our forebears embracing the Christian faith and the principles therein.

In my analysis and research, I studied the different spheres of our society. My studies covered politics and government, religion and the Church, family, economy, media and the educational sphere. I clearly pointed out that the national reformation, greatness and prosperity which occurred in Britain were mostly as a result of men and women transformed through the Gospel of Jesus Christ influencing these spheres.

I further contend that the spiritual, moral and commercial decline is directly attributable to the abandonment of this faith. Thus the title of my book, *Great Britain Has Fallen.*

In my second book *Awake Great Britain* (published by New Wine Press) I highlighted one strategic reason for moral failure, social decadence and economic malaise in the chapter titled A Case for Christianity In Schools. The reason was the Humanist Agenda championed by Alice Bailey.

In this present work, I would like to shed more light on Alice Bailey and her writings. The aim is to draw attention to how she has reversed most of the spiritual gains our forebears won for us.

---

119   *Great Britain Has Fallen*, Wale Babatunde, pp 18, 19, New Wine Press

History at Work

I am a lover of history, and an avid one at that. History not only educates us but informs, inspires us and chronicles the personalities involved, what accrued and the reasons behind them. History, therefore, teaches us how to face the future, particularly if we correctly understand its interpretations.

Reading through the life and writings of Alice Bailey has been an enlightening experience for me. But before I delve into the person of Alice Bailey, allow me take you on a background journey of a related personality to her story, Helena Blavatsky.

Helena Blavatsky

Helena Blavatsky, (née Helena Petrovna Hahn) was born on the 12th of August 1831, in Ukraine. She died on the 8th of May 1891 in London.

She was a Russian spiritualist, author, and cofounder of the Theosophical Society. The society was founded in New York City in 1875 with the motto, "There is no Religion higher than Truth." She defined Theosophy as,

> *"the archaic Wisdom-Religion, the esoteric doctrine once known in every ancient country having claims to civilization."*[120]

Blavatsky's extensive research into the many different spiritual traditions of the world led to the publication of what is now considered her magnum opus, *The Secret Doctrine*. Blavatsky is most well known for her promulgation of a theosophical system of thought, often referred to under various names, including

---

120 *The Theosophist,* Volume I, page 89

The Occult Science, The Esoteric Tradition, The Wisdom of the Ages, etc., or simply as Occultism or Theosophy.

She saw herself as a missionary of this ancient knowledge and one of the main purposes of the Theosophical Society was "to form a nucleus of the Universal Brotherhood of Humanity, without distinction of race, creed, sex, caste or color". Blavatsky is a leading name in the New Age Movement.

According to her, theosophy is Divine Knowledge or Science. She further states that the divine being is certainly not "God" in the sense attached in our day to the term. Therefore, it is not "Wisdom of God," as translated by some, but Divine Wisdom such as that possessed by the gods. She also states that all real lovers of divine wisdom and truth had, and have, a right to the name of Theosophist. The term is many thousand years old.

Following Blavatsky's death, disagreements among prominent Theosophists caused a series of splits and several Theosophical Societies and Organizations emerged. As of 2011, Theosophy remains an active philosophical school with a presence in more than 50 countries around the world.[121]

Alice Bailey – Her Connection to Helena Blavatsky

In previous chapters we saw how William Tyndale was greatly influenced by the writings and works of Desiderius Erasmus. This influence spawned the translation of the Bible in a version that became more accessible. Subsequently, this initiative made the Bible to be in wider circulation across Britain through the edict of His Royal Highness King Henry VIII. We will now see how the works of Helena influenced Alice, and how this influence has spawned a movement that has put us under siege.

Alice Bailey was born in Manchester, England in 1880. Her parents both died when she was young. Raised by relatives in a protective environment, she had a very difficult and abusive marriage which eventually led her to raise three young daughters alone. She later moved from England to the United States of America.

Her first contact with the occult world was the same deceptive forces that had used Helena Blavatsky in establishing the Theosophical Society through English Tea ladies, who lived in California. These persons were deeply involved in the occult teachings of Theosophy.

Her abusive marriage, coupled with her confusion about the purpose of life, most likely paved way for her openness to the occult. According to her, she often neglected reading the Bible but would sit up in bed reading the secret doctrines of Theosophy at night. This secret fascination later transformed her into a master teacher and one of the most strategic channels of demonic influence our world has known in modern times.

She died on the 15th of December 1949, just 30 days after the 'the Tibetan' had finished writing through her.

Alice Bailey – Her Influence And Works

After Alice Bailey was born, the leadership to further the plans of Lucifer (Satan) via Theosophy were transferred to her. In 1915 she discovered the Theosophical Society and the work of Helena Petrovna Blavatsky. Years later, she became the President of the Theosophical Society. Without doubt, she was the most strategic in laying down the foundation of the New Age Movement.

One day she had a visitation from a spirit that introduced himself as Djwhal Khul – a spirit from Tibet. She described the majority of her work as having been telepathically dictated to her by this spirit which she called a Master of Wisdom. Initially referred to only as "the Tibetan", or by the initials "D.K.", the spirit was later identified as Djwhal Khul.

This spirit offered her great success, if she could yield herself to be used to cheat the nations of the world. She obliged in this regard, thereby offering herself to be used in the service of Satan. It should be noted that she has many writings touching on every sphere of society. By the time she died in 1949, she had written 24 books, a total of 10,409 pages, most of which were allegedly written through her spirit guide, the Tibetan.

She further founded the *Lucis Trust*, which until recently had its headquarters at United Nations Plaza in the United States of America.

Alice Bailey was anti-Jewish and Anti-Christian. The purpose of her writings was to give the world an alternative set of values. What is most important to us about Alice Bailey was her Ten-Point plan or strategy, which was meant to bring about a New World Order (NWO).

This plan was primarily directed at Europe, where Christianity had taken roots in most spheres of society at this time. For example, Britain is a Christian nation by law and most of her laws and institutions are founded on Christian principles. Before we look at the Ten-Point plan, let us first consider the diabolical plan for the hierarchy to precede and condition the world for the New Age or New World Order. This plan falls into three categories.

Preparatory
   1875-1890 Helena Blavatsky
   1891:Dr. Annie Besant

Intermediate
   1919-1949 Alice Bailey

Revelatory (after) 1975 to be revealed worldwide

◊ Radio & Television
◊ Major producers
◊ Politicians
◊ Religious leaders
◊ Businessmen e.g. multinationals
◊ Educational institutions

The plan dictated to her by demonic spirits covered seven major fields of work namely:

◊ Political
◊ Religious
◊ Educational
◊ Scientific
◊ Philosophical
◊ Psychological
◊ Economic

The ultimate objective of this plan is to dethrone God and Christianity.

According to Alice Bailey, if any nation adopted her Ten-Point plan, Christianity would become a thing of the past. I wonder whether you see what I see. I wonder whether you can hear the promptings of the Holy Spirit. Let me highlight at least two important things.

1. Did you notice that the writings of Alice Bailey so far covered have their sights on almost all the sevens spheres of society? Again, take a look at what the Revelatory Plan after 1975 covers and the seven major fields targeted.

    "Let him that hath hears hear what the spirit is saying to the church."

    (Revelation 2:7, KJV)

2. As will be seen from the Ten-Point plan, you will discover
    how the adoption of this strategy since the end of the
    Second World War gradually began to change Britain,
    from a nation built on Christian principles to a humanistic
    and atheistic nation. The same applies to other nations
    that have been impacted by Christian principles. They
    include the United States of America and Canada. African
    continent particularly those presently experiencing revival,
    and reformation, watch out! This is what I call *Reformation
    in Reverse* (emphasis mine).

3. Thirdly and possibly finally, we will observe how this
    cancer can be dealt with decisively. In medical science,
    the first step in treating disease is diagnosis. After careful
    diagnosis, the next step (depending on the symptoms and
    complaints) is prescription. As you read this book, are you
    concerned about changing the fortunes of Great Britain?
    Does your concern extend to any nation that the New Age
    has affected? My submission to you is this; *target the seven
    spheres of our society with the gospel of the Kingdom.*
    Herein lies the secret of national transformation.

The 10-Point Strategy

The purpose of this plan was to change Christian tradition or
to redeem the nations of Christian traditions. It's important that
we observe how much of these plans have been implemented
in our nation.

"TAKE GOD AND PRAYER OUT OF THE EDUCATIONAL SYSTEM"

Alice Bailey remarked,

> *"Change the curriculum to ensure that children are
> freed from the bondage of Christian culture."*

Until some decades ago, God and the Bible were at the centre of our educational system. Text books in Britain taught the basics of social and civic responsibility from a Christian ethical viewpoint. Children were taught to pray. The Bible was read out loud in schools. The Ten Commandments were memorized, which in those days established moral absolutes. This has all stopped. God and prayer have been legislated out of our schools. Have you noticed that to mention God or say that Jesus is the only way to Heaven is almost a sin under the guise that someone from another religion may be offended? This is all done in a nation that is supposedly a Christian nation. Have the New Age and Alice Bailey succeeded in infiltrating our educational sphere? Without doubt! Is this only limited to Britain? I don't think so; the same applies to the USA, Canada, South Africa and many European States. Are the modern-day apostles to the educational sphere taking note? (cf *Awake Great Britain*, chapter 8, pp 101-116).

"REDUCE PARENTAL AUTHORITY OVER THEIR CHILDREN"
She also said,

> *"Break the communication between parent and child so that parents do not pass on their Christian traditions to their children. Liberate children from the bondage of their parents' tradition."*

This plan has been vigorously followed in Britain through a number of laws. The Children's Act of 1989 is a valid example. The introduction to the Act states that the child's welfare shall be the court's paramount consideration and any suggestion that parents are, except in extreme circumstances, the best judges of that are nowhere to be found. This Act even allows a Local Authority to take a child into care where the child had a transient dispute with their parents (Source: Great Britain Has Fallen by Wale Babatunde, New Wine Press, page 75-76) Again has Alice Bailey's plan succeeded in infiltrating the family sphere? No doubt, it has.

"DESTROY THE JUDEO-CHRISTIAN FAMILY STRUCTURE OR THE TRADITIONAL CHRISTIAN FAMILY STRUCTURE." WHY?

"The structure is oppressive and that the family is the core of the nation. If you break the family, you break the nation. Liberate the people from the confines of this structure."

How was this objective to be achieved?

1. Promote sexual promiscuity: Young people were to be freed from the concept of premarital sex. They are free to indulge in an active sexual lifestyle, since sex is the highest joy in life. There should be no inhibitions in enjoying this experience. In addition, they should be proud of the experience. In other words, they should flaunt it.

2. Use the media: television, magazines, the internet and many more arms of the media industry coupled with all forms of advertising, promote sex. Have you noticed how outdoor advertising in Britain today sends subliminal sex messages through particular ranges of products like women's bras, for example? Have you also noticed the sex education agenda? (For further reading, read *Great Britain Has Fallen*, Chapter 3 and *Awake! Great Britain*, Chapter 8, both published by New Wine Press).

"IF SEX IS FREE, THEN MAKE ABORTION LEGAL AND ACCESSIBLE"

Alice Bailey further declared,

> "Build clinics for Abortion Health Clinics in schools.
> If people are going to enjoy the joy of sexual
> relationships, they need to be free of unnecessary fears.
> In other words, they should not be hampered with
> unwanted pregnancies."

Has Alice Bailey's plan succeeded in any way? All you need do is study the various government laws. One of such is the 1967 Abortion Act, which made abortion legal in Britain. In effect, it has led to abortion on demand. Statistics indicate 97% of abortions are performed on healthy babies. It's also worth noting that since this Act was passed, restraint has been removed on sexual behaviour in Britain.[122] Is it a surprise that Britain leads in teenage pregnancies and abortions in Europe?

"MAKE DIVORCE EASY AND LEGAL, FREE PEOPLE FROM THE CONCEPT OF MARRIAGE FOR LIFE"

As part of her writing, Alice Bailey wrote that love does wear out, and if it happens, people should not be held under Christian bondage that marriage is for life. Therefore they should be free to enter into other relationships. Today, over sixty years after Alice Bailey's writings, marriage is nothing but a contract between two people, often with the thought of opting out at the slightest opportunity.

Today, divorce has, unfortunately, become easy, thanks to Government laws and the inability of the Church to give a moral lead. At present the divorce rate in Britain is close to 50%.

---

122   *Great Britain Has Fallen*, Wale Babatunde, pp 76-79, New Wine Press

Not only have Alice Bailey's writings infiltrated our family structure, they have also impacted our government, including the Houses of Parliament and the Judiciary.

"MAKE HOMOSEXUALITY AN ALTERNATIVE LIFESTYLE"

Over sixty years ago, Alice Bailey wrote that since sex is the highest enjoyment for mankind, no one should be denied this pleasure. As such, there should not be any form of restriction, be it heterosexual, homosexual, incest or bestiality. The main proviso is that the two people consent.

All the gay propaganda and agenda in Britain and in most western nations find inspiration from the writings of Alice Bailey. Take a look at Britain today. You will agree with me that not only has the homosexual lifestyle become almost accepted behaviour, it has even received Parliamentary endorsement. It gets even messier; the Church of today is expected to bless gays and lesbians!

Take a close look at the various British governments' stance on homosexuality in the last fifty years and you will understand what I am trying to communicate. Observe guidelines of the Sheffield Education Authority which includes twelve-year old pupils being taught the right to have sex with partners of their choice. Another example was Tony Blair's new Labour Agenda to lower the age of homosexual consent to sixteen from their move to repeal the section 28 of the Local Government Act (See *Great Britain Has Fallen*, pp 68-72).

"DEBASE ART"

What was Alice Bailey's strategy or plan in debasing art? It was a very simple plan. New forms of art which corrupt and defile the imagination of people were to be released. These include painting, music, drama, etc. Has she succeeded at all? Take a look at the kind of music, drama and films that are being released today in different formats, cinema, DVD, Blu-ray. A high percent of such content can be classified as pure pornography. Did you notice that this is another important sphere of our society that the New Age has virtually captured? Any lessons for Reformers and Revivalists? I believe there are a lot.

"USE MEDIA TO PROMOTE AND CHANGE MINDSET"

Alice Bailey preached over sixty years ago that the greatest channel you need to use to change human attitudes is the media. Use the press, radio, TV and cinema. Has she been successful? Take a look first at those who control our media today. They are members of the New Age Movement! Again, take a close look at the content of our TV programmes; they mostly promote the New Age agenda from ridiculing everything Christian to promoting alternative sexual lifestyle, as being normal. A case in point is celebrities engaging in sex outside marriage.

In *Great Britain Has Fallen*, I took the BBC to task by accusing them of abandoning their foundational charter or principle which was taken from Philippians 4:8 and substituting it for horrific, violent and pornographic programmes. Gone are the days when they transmitted programmes that were lovely, pure, decent and of good report. Today they have fallen for the schemes, tricks and snares of Alice Bailey's plan! Has Alice Bailey been able to affect, impact and dominate the media sphere of British society? The answer is not far-fetched. Gone are the days when our founding fathers like Lord Reith laid the foundations of our premier Broadcasting House, the BBC, on Christian principles. Things have changed since then. This is what I call *Reformation in Reverse*. For the apostles to the media, a word is enough for the wise!

"CREATE AN INTERFAITH MOVEMENT"

In other words, create another Babylon. Alice Bailey wrote,

> *"Promote other faiths to be at par with Christianity and break this thing about Christianity as being the only way to Heaven. By that, Christianity will be pulled down and other faiths promoted."*

Take a look at our nation, and you will see the fruits of this plan. The inter-faith movement is now rife. Other faiths, including Islam, have been greatly promoted in a so-called Christian nation at the expense of Christianity. While we must be proud of our tradition of religious freedom and tolerance, I have often raised this issue. Can the kind of freedom we extend to peoples of other faiths in Britain (which to my knowledge is still a Christian nation by Law) also be extended to Christians from Britain in Muslim countries like Iran and Saudi Arabia?

Again, this strategy is primarily directed towards the religious sphere, to diffuse our religious radicalism and neutralize our faith and call to witness.

"GET GOVERNMENTS TO MAKE ALL THESE LAWS AND GET THE CHURCH TO ENDORSE THESE CHANGES"

Alice Bailey further wrote that the Church must change its doctrine and accommodate the people by accepting these things and put them into its structures and systems.

In the chapter titled 'Britain's Unrighteous Government' from my book, Great Britain Has Fallen, I highlighted various ungodly laws that have been passed in our Houses of Parliament that were once founded upon Christian principles. Some of these laws in my own estimation couldn't have been passed by a right thinking, Bible-believing, God-fearing and patriotic members of Parliament. I have always wondered why our Parliament and our politicians seem to (in the words of our very own outspoken prophet now in glory David. E. Gardner) legislate backwards! The answer is not farfetched! They are following the humanistic plan championed by Alice Bailey.

What is worse and very much distasteful is that the New Age has succeeded in infiltrating the Church. By this I am referring to the plans of the Babylonian Church being endorsed.

Take a look at some of the changes that have taken place in Britain and indeed most of Europe and North America. These ungodly changes and laws sponsored by the New Age Movement have been supported or endorsed by a wing of the Church.

Take for example the issue of homosexuality in Britain. What has been the attitude of the Church to this thorny issue? Has the Church been able to speak with one voice? Why did you think the Anglican Church in Africa being led by Nigeria has threatened to break away from the Anglican Church in Britain? It's simply because the Church in Britain has compromised her doctrine. They have been taken over by the New Age agenda or propaganda.

Has Alice Bailey succeeded at all? I would say very much so. She has virtually brought about a New World Order bent on dethroning God and making Christianity a thing of the past, particularly in Europe and North America. Africa be warned! I see the New Age infiltrating media, business and commerce, education and government spheres. The next few decades will be very critical for the African continent. The only solution that will stem the tide be it in Britain, Western Europe, North America or even Africa is for the Church to begin to vigorously preach and live the gospel of the Kingdom.

> "And this gospel of the kingdom shall be preached in all the world for a witness unto all nations, and then shall the end come."
>
> (Matthew 24:14, KJV)

This is the only solution to attacking, neutralising and overcoming the reverse reformation been championed by Satan's apostles to change all the seven spheres of our society, Alice Bailey's plan in particular.

A Land Under Siege

In chapter four, we looked at the mandate given to two individuals, Loren Cunningham and Bill Bright. This mandate was further elaborated in Johnny Enlow's book, *The Seven Mountains Prophecy*, seven Old Testament nations that Israel was meant to conquer. In present times, these nations represent Media (Hittites); Government (Girgashites); Education (Amorites); Economy (Canaanites); Religion (Perizzites); Celebration; arts, music, sports, fashion entertainment (Hivites) and Family (Jebusites).[123]

We also observed how the great personalities who made Great Britain great achieved their respective vision; they operated with deep understanding of what the Kingdom of God is. They lived it. The society they found themselves in was under siege of darkness from vice, evil and, in some cases, death.

However, they knew their Saviour; they radiated light in the midst of the darkness they found themselves in. In addition, they were strategic at their work, mission and calling. There was a call to duty. They rose up to the challenge. The enemy was advancing towards the gates with full force.

Strategic Warfare

"In that day the LORD of hosts will be for a crown of
    glory
and a diadem of beauty to the remnant of His people,
For a spirit of justice to him who sits in judgment, and
    for strength
to those who turn back the battle at the gate."
(Isaiah 28:5-6, NKJV)

123 *The Seven Mountains Prophecy*, Johnny Enlow, Creation House, Florida, USA, 2008

Throughout the history of man, battles have been fought and won. In the 21st century, battles still rage all over the world. In biblical times, strategic strongholds were defined by high walls that were very fortified. These strongholds were usually cities, where the king and seat of government were situated. Different military strategies and tactics were employed towards taking these cities. One of such strategies was laying a siege round the city under attack. Opposing armies seeking to take such cities would camp round the walls of the cities, with a strategic location at the city gates (II Kings 6:1-8, Joshua 6:1, Judges 9:50). In certain cases, the siege paid off. In some others, however, it failed.

Today, we are faced with such a siege, no less. Just as in the days of old, the siege is successful in some areas, while being foiled in others. Nevertheless, it is relenting.

In the scripture above, the prophet Isaiah captures the relentless advance of the enemy's forces. He indicates a particular turn in the tide of the battle which will happen at the gates, the most strategic part of a city's fortifications. But, he gives a reassuring word. For those who will turn the battle at the gates, there is strength from above. In effect, we are also meant to be relentless in our mandate to establish God's Kingdom on earth.

Empowered for Greatness

> "Arise, shine, for your light has come, and the glory of the LORD shines over you."
>
> (Isaiah 60:1, Holman Christian Standard Bible)

This scripture gives me a lot of spiritual vigour and gusto. My main reason is because it is a recurrent wakeup call for any situation I find myself in. Wherever I may be that gives me cause for alarm, or whatever issue that it is knocking at my door, I have been divinely empowered to resolve the matter without any fear of failure or defeat. Of particular interest is the word 'glory'. In Hebrew, it is translated as 'chabod' and occurs in the Strong's Concordance Dictionary (#3519). It implies the following: honour, splendour, power, wealth, authority, magnificence, fame, dignity, riches, fame and excellency. 'Chabod' is God's glory, not only His honour, but also His visible splendor. This then means that for as long as we operate in the light of God Almighty, radiating His glory, we demonstrate His attributes. These attributes were visible in the lives of the very great men and women who were sold out to the gospel and made Britain great in the process. The same attributes are available for us as long as we are committed to establishing the Kingdom of God on earth through His Word.

> *"Our bodies are made of clay, yet we have the treasure of the Good News in them. This shows that the superior power of this treasure belongs to God and doesn't come from us."*
>
> (II Corinthians 4:7, GOD'S WORD Translation)

Our society is under siege. What are we doing about it? Misleading and discouraging influences have become the order of the day. What is our response? The gates of our homes, lives, families, values are under relentless and persistent cycles of sieges. How are we combating these attacks?

The Seven Mountain Strategy gives us a blueprint on how we can operate within the rank and file of God's army. As we continually seek to establish His Kingdom on earth to the glory of His name, we thereby restore the greatness this country was once identified with. We have the Light of God (our Father in Heaven) in us and His glory upon us.

The great individuals outlined in previous chapters took specific stands, maintained their stand and turned back the battle at the very gates the sieges were laid. Our Father in Heaven expects us to do nothing less.

THE JOURNEY AHEAD

29 *LESSONS IN HISTORY*

||||||||||||||||||||||||||||||||| |||||||||||||||||||||||||||||||||||||||||||||||||||||||||||||||||||||||||||||||||||

> *"We are assured and know that [God being a partner in their labour] all things work together and are [fitting into a plan] for good to and for those who love God and are called according to [His] design and purpose."*
>
> (Romans 8:28, The Amplified Bible)

> *"Now all these things happened to them as examples and they were written for our admonition, upon whom the ends of the ages have come."*
>
> (I Corinthians 10:11, NKJV)

Someone might rightly enquire, *what use is studying about the past particularly the lives of those who have made an indelible mark on our society? After all, the past is better left behind, in the past. We should rather concern ourselves with the present.*

The study of history has always been a profitable venture. History informs us about an earlier period, what happened, the reasons why it occurred. It also informs us about important personalities, why they became great and how they changed the course of history. History serves to inspire, encourage, and make us understand one particular fact; history-makers and world changers are not super human.

Furthermore, the study of history helps coming generations to be mentored by others, albeit by people they never met or encountered. As we glean through their lives (tragedies and triumphs, weaknesses and strengths), our faith can be mentored by their stories.

Also, by studying the lives of these sterling personalities, we get a better feel of the ideas many of them conceived in order to change their communities, cities and nations. Future generations can, as a result, be inspired to develop our communities and nation.

After all, as the wise man Solomon proclaimed,

> *"...there is nothing new under the sun"*
>   (Ecclesiastes 1:9, NKJV)

So what specific lessons can we learn from the stories of men and women we have encountered so far in this book? Truth be told, the heroes and heroines chronicled in this book all have unique stories. Nevertheless, there are peculiarities unique to most of them, if not all.

Sense Of Destiny Or Purpose

One common thread that runs through the lives of the men and women that we have encountered throughout this book is that they all nursed a deep sense of destiny or purpose. They almost knew, without a shadow of doubt, God's hand rested upon their lives for a unique purpose. This is one of the key reasons why they changed their world and left an indelible mark on the sands of time.

William Wilberforce, social reformer and politician from Hull, declared that he believed there were two major assignments that God reposed on him; first was the reformation of manners and second the abolition of the slave trade.

Charles Haddon Spurgeon, the *Prince of Preachers*, commented on what he believed to be a divine mandate on his life to train pastors and church leaders. He once remarked,

> *"My first born and best beloved. This is my life's work, to which I believe God has called me, therefore I must do it."*

This is an indispensable characteristic or trait of would-be world changers and history makers. Paul, the Great Apostle, also possessed such a clear sense of destiny. Once he remarked,

> *"Yet when I preach the gospel, I cannot boast, for I am compelled to preach. Woe to me if I do not preach the gospel!"*
>
> (I Corinthians 9:16, NIV)

Again, Paul recounting his divine mandate and mission before King Agrippa, declared,

> *"So then, King Agrippa, I was not disobedient to the vision from heaven."*
>
> (Acts 26:19, NIV)

Do you want to change your world? Are you passionate about leaving a lasting legacy like the heroes of our faith? You must have a crystal-clear sense of destiny and purpose.

Risk Takers

> *"And there were four leprous men at the entering in of the gate: and they said one to another, Why sit we here until we die?*

> *If we say, We will enter into the city, then the famine*
> *is in the city, and we shall die there: and if we sit still*
> *here, we die also. Now therefore come, and let us fall*
> *unto the host of the Syrians: if they save us alive, we*
> *shall live; and if they kill us, we shall but die."*
> (2 Kings 7:3-4 KJV)

I once heard a preacher declare that faith is a risk, and it is risky not to take a risk. Another indispensable trait of world-changers (men and women who have changed British history) is that they were risk takers. Observe closely the four leprous men at the entrance of the gate of Samaria. They had to take a great risk before they discovered an abundance of food, drink, silver, gold and clothes.

Our heroes and heroines were confronted with almost impossible tasks and situations. Many of them put their lives on the line in the course of serving God, fellow citizens and their nation.

As I read the stories and exploits of David Livingstone in the jungles of Africa, I cannot but salute his courage and will.

How could he have walked several hundred miles, often encountering hostile and tribal men? At other times, their lives were exposed to dangerous animals. For example, David Livingstone was once mauled by a lion. Yet, rather than give up on his mission, this attack fired his resolve.

Read the history of the exploits of the Queen of Calabar, Mary Slessor, and you cannot help being amazed at her tenacity of purpose. She would trek into the dangerous bush to rescue banished twins and sometimes mediate between warring factions and villages.

Even as an African, born on the soil of Africa, I would still find it difficult to travel to many places today let alone about a hundred and fifty years ago.

Passion For Learning And Education

Without exception, all the men and women that have become heroes in Britain were people who had a great desire and passion for learning and education. They saw the correlation between fulfilment of their destinies and a life given to diligent study.

Paul, the erudite scholar from Tarsus, writing to his protégé from the prison in Rome, charged Timothy to devote or give himself wholly to learning, because in doing this, his profiting would appear to all men.

> *"Till I come give attention to reading."*
>   (1 Timothy 4:13, NKJV)

Despite working fourteen hours a day from the age of ten, David Livingstone still managed to enrol in evening classes. In our day, when young people earn their first pay, they spend it on clothing, partying or pleasure. What did Livingstone do? He bought a Latin grammar book, showing his strong passion and desire for learning. This is a great lesson for all those who desire to impact and change their sphere of influence in society.

John Wesley, on his part, formed a group with his colleagues. They all belonged to the Holy Club and were graduates of Oxford University, a testament to their passion for education. Furthermore, the travelling evangelists under John Wesley and the Methodist movement were charged to carry certain books. These books were meant to be studied and referred as recommended texts for members and new converts.

Thomas Sydenham was known as the father of English Medicine. On his part, he schooled at both Oxford and Cambridge, two of the best citadels of learning in the country.

Are you a young person? As you read this book, can I challenge you to do everything possible to make sure that you give yourself completely to learning? There is always rewarding fruit attached to it. Anyone who will ever excel in their chosen field or sphere of influence must make sure that they are on top of their game.

My watchword to my children and students is this: education, education, education.

Age is never a barrier for learning. Even if you are well advanced in years, as long as you have discovered your life's mission and sphere of influence, give yourself to rigorous study on a daily basis. Enrol in relevant educational institutions that will sharpen you to become the best.

Suffering and Sacrifice

One common characteristic that I have also discovered is they all achieved this extraordinary feat at great cost. In studying the lives of these men and women, it becomes obvious how they changed the socio-political as well as economic and spiritual climate of their communities. They further impacted our nation and the world at large. However, they had to pay the price. Never did anyone become a world changer without having paid the price.

Often this price cost them relationships with their families. In many cases, weeks, months and often years passed without the company of their most loved ones. At other times, they suffered the loss of their spouses and children.

Like Paul in the Bible, many denied themselves marriage in order to give tunnel-vision to their life's mission. A few of them even paid the ultimate price with their lives in pursuit of what they felt was a divine mandate.

Many sold their personal possessions, denied themselves pleasures and the affection of their families, like Charles Spurgeon, in order to build a lasting legacy. Anyone conversant with the history of the Slave Trade Abolition Campaign championed by William Wilberforce will agree with me that it came at a great price. Not only was he ostracized together with his group by close friends and colleagues, they further met with great opposition from members of the British Parliament.

Often, they had to deny themselves sleep in order to gather much needed data to defeat the opposition in Parliament.

William Tyndale also paid the ultimate price when he was burnt at the stake. His crime was making the Bible accessible to the common man.

I am often shocked by Christian leaders, some of whom I relate with, who complain about the persecutions that they encounter. They particularly recount when they are called names they find distasteful and disturbing.

My advice is always simply to go and read the biographies of some of the names mentioned in earlier chapters of this book. Then can we really be grateful for the seemingly light affliction that we are passing through. It is my considered opinion that in the present-day 21st century we have few history makers because many people are unwilling to pay the price required.

Read your Bible and you will understand this; anyone who will truly follow Christ and stand for the truth will do so at great cost.

The Man from Nazareth declares,

> "If anyone desires to come after Me, let him deny himself, and take up his cross and follow me."
>
> (Matthew 16:24, NKJV)

Friend, do you want your life to count in your community and, ultimately, nation? Then be prepared to sacrifice all, including your life.

I have been privileged to fellowship with one of God's Generals of our days, Pastor Sunday Adelaja of the Embassy of God in Ukraine. I am amazed at how a man born in a village in far away Nigeria could have positively impacted a former Communist enclave.

I got the answer when one day he declared unequivocally that he was ready to lay down his life for the cause of Christ. This, in my opinion, is the secret of greatness.

Social Responsibility

A few years ago, I was privileged to travel to Liberia, a former American colony in West Africa. I was in the company of the Duchess of York, Sarah Ferguson, and a few other trustees of a charity that I was part of. Our mission was to go and open some schools for deserving children who had lost their parents in the civil war that engulfed the nation for over a decade.

During one of the ceremonies, some girls came to perform. I remember very vividly, towards the end of their cultural dance, how a girl stepped forward and pointed at the audience. It was as if she singled me out. In her young but firm voice she said, "You have not changed anything until you have changed lives".

This left an indelible impression on my heart. Indeed, as Christians, we have a social responsibility to be our brother's keeper, in a nutshell, to make the world a better place. We are to be the Good Samaritan, who offered a helping hand to a fellow pilgrim in dire need. I would never have studied the lives of these great men and women had they lived only for themselves and their families. They would have been long forgotten if they did not champion the cause of the poor, stood up for the underprivileged, marginalized and the common good of the masses.

Study the life of Elizabeth Fry. Consider the sacrifice of Florence Nightingale. Explore the stories of John Howard. One thing is common to them all. They lived for the improved welfare of their fellow citizens. William Booth is one of my heroes. I am always inspired by the motto of the Salvation Army, *Heart to God and Hand to Man.*

To William Booth and the Salvation Army, there was no dichotomy; neither between spiritual work nor social gospel. Both were meant to go hand in hand. Good news to the poor is not only preaching the gospel; but feeding and housing them as well.

Any lessons for the 21st century Church? I believe there are lots of lessons. We need to begin channelling more of our efforts and resources towards ministering to the physical and practical needs of our community. After all, the Good Man from Nazareth not only preached like many of us do today, but He also fed the multitudes with food.

We must give respect to many of the traditional or mainline Churches for the social work they have done over the centuries. The Baptists, Anglicans, Methodists, and Roman Catholics (to mention a few), have been involved in projects like housing, feeding, education, (vocational) training etc.

It must also be mentioned that many of the new Pentecostal and Charismatic Churches in Britain are beginning to take their place. Two good examples of social responsibility which immediately come to mind are The Street Pastors championed by Les Isaac and The Peace Alliance, led by Pastor Nims Obunge.

However, it must be said that a lot still needs to be done, particularly from my brethren and denominations in Africa.

I always remind myself that when the missionaries came to Africa, their activities were not just limited to the planting of churches and the conversion of people to Christianity.

They were involved in ministries and projects that benefited the community and nation at large. Such endeavours, included schools, hospitals and training centres!

Powered By Prayer

As you read through the stories and exploits of these great men and women who made Great Britain great, you will likely be inspired by their achievements and challenged by their extraordinary feats.

To the spiritually naïve or undiscerning, these men and women achieved so much simply because of their education, drive and the willingness to pay the sacrifice for success. While all these may be true, I have also discovered that one indispensable quality which was responsible for their success is their dependence on the power of prayer.

Almost without exception, all the projects, initiatives and ministries these reformers and revivalists were involved with were first conceived, sustained and executed in the womb of prayer.

Elizabeth Fry, the Prison Reformer, was not only a woman wholly given to prayer; she prayed and read the Bible daily with all the prison inmates she visited. The Great Awakening led by John Wesley was birthed and sustained in the place of prayer.

In fact, the national transformation that ensued from this Awakening could only have been possible because of men and women who gave themselves to earnest and heartfelt prayer.

In a time when Christian prayers are gradually being marginalized and legislated against, it may surprise many of us that daily prayers were part of the curriculum in most of our educational institutions at their inception. Such institutions included Oxford, Cambridge and Eton College, to mention a few.

All the men of science were men of the Word and prayer. Both Mary Slessor and Florence Nightingale were women totally given to prayer.

Any lessons for us today? I wholeheartedly believe that the single most important reason why Britain is in a critical state, spiritually and morally, is because of the apathy of the Church to pray.

Today, there is darkness all over the land and gross darkness over the people, because there is paucity of prayers!

There is so much talk about prayer in the Church today that we have little time left for actually praying. We strategize, complain about the state of the nation, but end up doing little or no praying. The curse of this hour is a prayer-less Church.

"The pastor who is not praying is playing; the people who are not praying are straying. Poverty stricken as the church is today in many things, she is most stricken here, in the place of prayer.

We have many organizers but few prayers; many players and payers, few prayers; many singers, few clingers; lots of pastors, few wrestlers, many fears, few tears. Many interferers, few intercessors. Failing here, we fail everywhere."[124]

Needed in this critical hour are 'prayers' and 'more prayers'.

The Sovereignty of God

> "What shall we say then? Is there unrighteousness with God? God forbid.
> For he saith to Moses, I will have mercy on whom I will have mercy, and I will have compassion on whom I will have compassion.
> So then it is not of him that willeth, nor of him that runneth, but of God that sheweth mercy."
>
> (Romans 9:14-16, KJV)

One of the clearest lessons I have learnt in studying the lives of the history makers mentioned in this book is the demonstration of God's sovereignty. There was always grace at work!

No doubt, the choice of these men and women can be nothing but divine in origin. Quite often, God chooses the least, the last and the lost. They were not always individuals who had it all together.

The basis for the choice of such persons could be drawn from the scripture below,

> "For ye see your calling, brethren, how that not many wise men after the flesh, not many mighty, not many noble, are called:
> But God hath chosen the foolish things of the world to confound the wise; and God hath chosen the weak

124   *Why Revival Tarries*, Leonard Ravenhill, Bethany Books, Minneapolis,1959

things of the world to confound the things which
  are mighty;
And base things of the world, and things which are
  despised, hath God chosen, yea, and things which
  are not, to bring to nought things that are:
That no flesh should glory in his presence."
                                    (I Corinthians 1:26-29, KJV)

Furthermore, I also discovered that their lives had been at serious risk. Had there been no divine intervention, their lives would have been lost and their assignments terminated.

Indeed the sovereignty of God was at work. I have always wondered how James the leader of the early Church was killed and yet Peter was spared (Acts 12). I am still baffled at how many Hebrew children in Egypt were killed in the genocide policy of Pharaoh, yet Moses survived in a basket of bulrushes in the Nile River (Exodus 2:1-10).

My only plausible answer is the demonstration of the sovereignty of God. It is God superimposing His divinity upon humanity.

How do you explain the timely rescue of the five year old John Wesley from an inferno which should have burnt him to death? The inferno itself was caused by his father's uncouth parishioners who set fire to the Epworth rectory located in the swampy fens of Lincolnshire. If this was not the sovereignty of God, I cannot fathom what else it may have been.

Little wonder that John's mother, Susanna Wesley, exclaimed quoting the Bible,

"Surely this is a brand plucked out of the burning!"

I can only attribute this deliverance to the work of the Holy God preserving the vessel, as Moses was preserved and would later bring about change in the life of a nation!

When I read the stories and exploits of David Livingstone, and what he did for Britain and indeed the African continent, I can also attribute his timely recue from the jaws of a lion in Africa as the handiwork of the God of Heaven preserving him, because of the strategic assignment placed on his shoulders.

Have you been delivered and preserved by God from a rare debilitating disease? Have you been involved in an automobile accident that killed everyone in the car or plane crash and yet you survived?

Did the doctors once give up on you or have you faced some unusual circumstances, attacks, persecutions, sufferings? Often, the above scenarios give an indication of what lies ahead of you. There's a weight of glory that you are carrying for your generation. Don't give up. Rejoice. Arise, because all these light afflictions are nothing to be compared to the weight of Glory to be received at the second coming of Jesus Christ.

30 *CAN BRITAIN EVER BE GREAT AGAIN?*

|||||||||||||||||||||||||||||||||||||||||||||||||||||||||||||||||||||||||||||||||||||||||||||||||||||||||||||

"The price of greatness is responsibility."
Winston Leonard Spencer Churchill (1874-1965)

"Righteousness exalts a nation, but sin is a disgrace to any people."
(Proverbs 14:34, New Living Translation)

In natural seasons there are cycles. Winter, Summer, Autumn, Spring. The beginning of one marks the end of another. We have seen how situations in Great Britain were in a deplorable condition. Then, the social and spiritual reformers stepped in. Now it seems as if the pendulum has swung back. In the light of all these, one of the fundamental questions engaging the minds of many today is whether or not Great Britain will ever be great again? To many, the glory, fame and greatness that this nation once enjoyed among the family of Nations has fizzled out. International politics and relations have changed. The world has moved on.

Events have been determined by new and emerging trends. In this modern age, we as a people should simply be thankful for our heritage.

There are, however, still some sterling individuals scattered all across this nation. They are not only burdened and disappointed at the present state of things, but receive their

265

encouragement from the "good old days". They are also inspired by other great personalities who have been instrumental in bringing greatness to this nation.

Often I have had the opportunity of meeting with some in prayer meetings. They would lie on their faces crying out to God for the land, others I have met in Parliament, trying to speak out for righteousness. Some are in the media, in education, often anonymous and common folk in our nation.

So what kind of greatness are we talking about? Some see Britain's greatness as her influence among the nations, others a time when we imagine there will be so much prosperity in the nation that the elderly, weak, children and the socially marginalized will be well taken care of. However the greatness that the author is speaking about is greatness that is devoid of exploitation. It is not greatness that is linked to colonialism or Empire.

True greatness is only of God. For no nation can be great apart from knowing and honouring Jesus Christ in the lives of individuals and as a nation. I sincerely believe that Great Britain can once again be great.

I speak of a time when there will be great revival touching and transforming the Church, waking the Church from dead religion, apathy and formalism. I speak of a time when true New Testament Christianity will be restored. The resultant effect will be mass of changed individuals who will, in turn, bring about a transformation of our society.

When I speak of a time our nation was truly great, I refer to the days of the Great Awakening in the 18th century. The Wesleyan Revival had a far-reaching impact both in this nation and abroad. The Missionary Movement that came out of this nation and took the Gospel of grace to the ends of the earth came as a result of this revival. During this time, we began to model our nation in line with biblical principles. Our fame also spread both far. The whole of our society was radically transformed. This is the kind of greatness that I envisage.

This is the kind of transformation that we are praying and hoping for.

Let us observe a few testimonies about the effect of this 18th century revival that brought greatness to our nation and be inspired.

Writing of the revival's far-reaching effects, Trevelyan, in his British History of the 19th century, states,

> *"It was one of the turning points in the history of the world."*

This he said of Britain after she had abolished the slave trade.

> *"Her command of the sea, her Far-Flung Empire, her mounting industrial power, her commercial supremacy, her inventive genius – above all, her increasing moral stature, and her expanding spiritual vision won her a place of unique leadership amongst the nations. More than any other great nation in the middle of the 19th century she was worthy of world power."*[125]

Furthermore, as a result of this revival the British people became known all over the world as "The People of The Book", and that book was the Bible. It was directly due to the influence of this same revival that it was being said all over the World at this time that "an Englishman's word is to be trusted, his word is his bond".

The Only Way to Greatness – The Church

We have traced the chronicles of how Britain attained greatness in ages past. What I am about to say may offend some people,

125   *The Trumpet Sounds for Great Britain*, Vol 1, David E Gardner, p 96, Christian Foundation Publications, Cheshire UK, 1980

but this is the truth. Debates and more debates in Parliament will not change this nation. Bringing more policemen to our streets will never change the heart of men. Writing protest letters or demonstrating will not turn this nation from its present moral and spiritual bankruptcy. Interfaith dialogue or joint communiqués will do nothing to our land.

The key to the change is in the hands of the Church. There are no sustainable solutions to our nation's problems outside of the Church. I pray that the Church will grasp this fact sooner than later. I hope Christian leaders all across this island will heed this counsel.

Jesus declared during His earthly ministry,

> *"I am the light of the world."*
>
> *(John 8:12, NKJV)*

However, in the same vein He looked at his disciples, His followers and declared to them;

> *"You are the light of the world."*
>
> *(Matthew 5:14, NKJV)*

It is light that dispels darkness. Light brings clarity, light ushers in change.

This name will become great again, when the Church wakes up. Great Britain will become great again, when the Church becomes desperate for God. At the moment, we have substituted God with programmes, personalities, denominationalism, pleasures, leisure and the like.

We will become great again when we deal with sin from the roots, when we identify sin for what it really is, sin and not something else.

We must deal with sin in the camp. We must break down all the barriers that have divided the Church, including divisions along racial lines, "The Black Church, the White Church, the Asian Church, the Caribbean Church" and all the other nomenclatures foreign to the New Testament.

We must do away with the Church that is built on social discrimination, upper class, middle class, working class, etc.

We must begin to see ourselves as one.

> "Do not lie to one another, since you have put off the old man with his deeds, and have put on the new man who is renewed in knowledge according to the image of Him who created him, where there is neither Greek nor Jew, circumcised nor uncircumcised, barbarian, Scythian, slave nor free, but Christ is all and in all."
>
> (Colossians 3:9-11, NKJV)

Yes, the key towards Revival and Reformation is in the hands of the Church, because the promise of healing the land is only given by God to His covenant people.

> "If my people, who are called by my name, will humble themselves and pray and seek my face and turn from their wicked ways, then will I hear from heaven and will forgive their sins and will heal their land."
>
> (2 Chronicles 7:14, KJV)

Humble Ourselves

Let no one be deceived. Before we experience revival, reformation and true greatness in our land, we must fulfil the conditions attached to this scripture. First, we must humble ourselves. This is the great need today. There's so much spiritual pride and arrogance today in the Church. From the pulpit to the pew, we have people who are so full of themselves. O God! In your mercy help us to humble ourselves or humiliate us (if need be) and then restore us.

Pray And Seek God's Face

I have attended too many so-called prayer meetings that were everything but prayer meetings. We chatted, argued on issues, discussed about the state of the Church and nation, exchanged business cards and in our custom, drank loads of tea and coffee. Yet, we barely prayed.

Leonard Ravehill succinctly describes the prayerlessness of the Church today when he writes,

> *"Poverty stricken as the church is today in many things, she is most stricken here, in the place of prayer. We have many organizers, but few agonisers, many players and payers, few prayers many singers, few clingers, lots of pastors, few wrestlers, many fears, few tears much fashion, little passion, any interferers few intercessors, many writers, but few fighters failing here, we fail everywhere."[126]*

It was Matthew Henry who made the remark,

> *"When God intends great mercy for his people, the first thing he does is set them a-praying."[127]*

Because, God intends to show great mercy to this nation, the cry of the Spirit to the Church in this nation is a **CALL TO PRAYER**! By this I mean heartfelt, agonizing, society-transforming prayers. We have seen these kind of prayers in the transformation videos on Cali-South America, Uganda and more recently, Nigeria. May God send us to our knees.

126 *Why Revival Tarries,* Leonard Ravehill, p 19
127 Ibid, p 21

Turn From Our Wicked Ways

This is the last condition that we must fulfil, before we can expect heaven to respond with mercy. I don't believe God's main problem in this country is with the sins of those who don't know Jesus as Lord and personal Saviour. After all, what do you expect from a sinner? To sin, that's their nature. The matter God sees as a problem is this: His people who live in sin with reckless abandon. Sin must be judged in the camp. As long as Israel obeyed and followed God's laws, statutes and instructions, they lived in prosperity, peace and defeated all their enemies. However, as soon as idolatry, immorality or any other sin was allowed in their midst, defeat and shame were inevitable.

Let us go back to our history and be instructed. Let us consult the ancients and the wise. True greatness only came to this nation when changed men changed our nation. This is our prayer for this hour. This is a plea. This is our desire. May Great Britain be great again! God bless Great Britain! Amen!

We hope you enjoyed reading this
New Wine book.
For details of other New Wine books
and a wide range of titles from other
Word and Spirit publishers visit our website:
www.newwineministries.co.uk
or email us at newwine@xalt.co.uk